MICHEL
ROUX
AT HOME

MICHEL ROUX

ROUX

AT HOME

My favourite recipes for family and friends

SEVEN DIALS

CONTENTS

Introduction

The food in this book really is what I cook and eat with my family, particularly when I'm at my house in France. It's the food I was brought up on and that we as a family enjoy. French home cooking is very different from fine dining restaurant food. Like Italian cooking, it's all about using good seasonal ingredients and letting them shine by not messing around with them too much. And that's exactly what I do at home, whether I'm cooking for myself and my wife Gisèle or for friends and family. I'm not into fuss or fancy frills. Our meals are often just one course, always followed by a little something sweet – even if it's only a couple of squares of dark chocolate.

In France I shop at the markets, but when in London I go to the local shops as much as possible. I'm lucky that near my house I have a good greengrocer, fishmonger and butcher, all just a few minutes' walk away. Whether at the market or the local London shops, I seldom set out with an exact idea of what I'm going to cook. I prefer to be inspired by what looks good on the day. Perhaps I'll see some beautiful fresh mackerel and decide to enjoy it simply grilled. Then at the greengrocer's I might find some new season's asparagus – a perfect accompaniment – and that's supper settled. On high days and holidays, though, I'm happy to spend a bit longer cooking something special for family and friends.

My family are originally from the north of France and Burgundy, where the cooking is rich in butter and cream, but these days I find myself gravitating much more to the food of the south, featuring olive oil and lots of fresh fruit and vegetables. My home in France is in the south, in the Ardèche, which is where my wife and her family are from, and that's my style of cooking now.

The beauty of using good, fresh, seasonal ingredients is that you don't have to do a lot to them. They speak for themselves. And I often save myself time and work by asking

the fishmonger to fillet and pin bone my fish, or the butcher
to joint a chicken. I'm happy to use ingredients such as jars
of roasted peppers and chargrilled artichokes, too. They're
amazing products – someone else has done the hard work
for you, and they have done it well. I don't make my own puff
pastry either and I'm a great fan of frozen peas. Also, meat
or fish don't always have to be the stars of a meal. For me,
it's not so much a case of meat and a little veg but the other
way round. I like the flavour that a bit of meat or fish brings
to a meal, but you don't need a lot. I love my vegetables.

Most of the recipes in this book are straightforward and give
maximum pleasure for minimum effort. When I'm at home
I don't have time to spend hours in the kitchen, and when I'm
on holiday I want to relax with my family. I'm sure you are the
same. There are some recipes in the book which take a bit more
time though and that can be fun too. The important thing is
to enjoy your cooking.

My tips for success in the kitchen are first, to buy the best
ingredients you can within your budget. And second, before you
start cooking, read the recipe through carefully and make sure
you have everything you need to hand. Get all the ingredients
and any equipment out ready. This is how professional cooks
work and it's a good idea at home too. Being organised in this
way makes you more efficient and less messy. Nothing in this
book demands anything special in the way of equipment –
no water baths, vac-packing machines or other fancy gadgets.
I've arranged my recipes into the following chapters.

BREAKFAST AND BRUNCH

Brunch-style breakfast has really taken off in France in recent
years. When I was growing up, brunch was seen as very much
an American thing. Breakfast for us, even at the weekend, was
coffee and a croissant. Now cafés and brasseries all over France
are offering some sort of brunch, including egg dishes, pancakes
and waffles, and it's hugely popular, as it is in Britain. At home
we do make an effort to have something a bit more special on
a Sunday. Anything with eggs is a favourite with me, such as the
omelette with anchovies (page 26) but I also enjoy making little

special treats, such as venison turnovers (page 28) and blue cheese sausage rolls (page 27), both of which you can prepare the night before and pop in the oven in the morning.

QUICK LUNCHES

If I'm at home, lunch for me is usually something I can rustle up with what's in the fridge or store cupboard. I like to sit down, look at my bowl of soup or salad and think, life is good! But quick doesn't mean junk food – lunch must be tasty, nutritious and filling. Soup is a favourite and I like to make a batch and enjoy it over several days. The French eat a lot of soup and there are infinite ways of making it interesting and delicious – for example, the watercress soup with poached egg and black pudding (page 46). Salad is another great lunch option, particularly in the summer, and lunch for my wife Gisèle and me is often a bowl of salad, with the addition of some leftovers or some ham or pâté or some store cupboard ingredients, such as peppers, anchovies or cheese. You'll find plenty of examples in this chapter.

SIMPLE SUPPERS FOR TWO

The dishes in this chapter are exactly the sort of food that Gisèle and I will sit down to in the evenings. I don't want to spend a lot of time making supper, even for my dear wife! We just want a simple meal we can share and enjoy with a glass or two of wine. In this chapter you will find several pasta recipes. In France we eat a lot of pasta, it's not only an Italian thing. I was brought up on pasta, so was my daughter, and my grandson thoroughly enjoys a pasta meal. It's a staple, particularly in southern France, and of course, it is a great vehicle for other ingredients and flavours. I often just look in the fridge and see what I can add to whatever pasta we have, but there are some special favourites here, such as the creamy onion tagliatelle (page 68), which is easy to make and a wonderfully comforting bowl of goodness. The linguine recipe on page 71 uses some great store cupboard ingredients, while the tagliolini with seafood (page 83) is a bit more work but is a really excellent supper for two. Fish is a great thing to cook for two of you – quick and easy. Try the cod and vegetable parcels (page 79), which you can prepare in advance, ready to cook in 20 minutes. Another regular is duck leg confit (page 90). I buy the duck confit, crisp it up in a pan and enjoy it with mushrooms and ready-peeled chestnuts – simple and delicious.

MEALS WITH FAMILY AND FRIENDS

These dishes are a bit more special and just the thing when you want to give people a bit of treat. Some do require a bit of work in the kitchen, while others might need a long cooking time. The pot-au-feu (page 145), for example, is simple to put together but does need to cook for a couple of hours. It's well worth the wait. I love slow-cooked meat, such as the spiced lamb (page 137), and these dishes are always better made the day before you want to eat them and reheated. This makes them ideal for entertaining, as you can get all the work out of the way and enjoy spending times with your guests on the day. Not all these recipes feature meat or fish. My wife and I think of ourselves as flexitarians and certainly don't eat meat every day of the week. I like to make some special vegetarian dishes, such as the quinoa salad (page 102) and the cauliflower and broccoli gratin (page 105) both of which are full of flavour and very filling.

SWEET FINISH

I do like a little something sweet at the end of a meal and this chapter contains some of the desserts that are popular with my family. Some, such as the coffee cream pots (page 171), are simple and take minutes to prepare, while others are more complex and require some time and effort in the kitchen, such as the blackberry and apple mille-feuilles (page 167). It will all be worthwhile when you see the pleasure on people's faces as they take a mouthful. I love to use seasonal fruits in desserts such as the strawberry and Maraschino cream (page 175). And in months when there are no fresh berries, I enjoy treats like the sabayon with glazed chestnuts (page 165) or pears in red wine (page 177). Chocolate is a favourite with all the family, so I had to include Grandma Roux's recipe for chocolate mousse (page 178), plus an indulgent dark chocolate tart (page 176).

FAMILY CELEBRATIONS AT HOME

This chapter features a special menu for each season, plus a Christmas menu, made up of many of our family favourites. The seasonal menus all have three courses, plus a little canapé to start the meal off while enjoying a glass of fizz or a cocktail. The Christmas menu has an extra course because – well, it's Christmas! The menus are designed to feature seasonal ingredients, be balanced, and to leave you sated and happy without feeling over full. And of course, you can use any of these dishes on their own. For instance, you might want to do a little buffet featuring all the canapés. Cooking a celebration meal will inevitably require some time and work but shouldn't be a chore. My advice is to get everyone involved to help out and do their bit, whether it's some peeling and chopping or just clearing up when it's all over.

KITCHEN BASICS

Many of these recipes are referred to earlier in the book and are part of your armoury as a home cook – recipes for sauces, such as hollandaise, salad dressings and classic accompaniments such as creamy mashed potatoes. You can buy good stocks now, but I have also included recipes for making your own if you wish. If you do buy stock, I recommend choosing the refrigerated ones which have fewer preservatives and to check the ingredients – a good stock should contain bones, veg, water and maybe a bit of wine but nothing else.

Some people still see French food as fine dining, haute cuisine, which of course it can be. But I hope the recipes in this book show that French home cooking doesn't have to be complicated, involving loads of ingredients and special techniques. It is simple, seasonal and achievable and shouldn't be a chore. Be spontaneous, be led by the wonderful ingredients you see and feel free to adapt recipes to what is available.

I believe that if you relax and enjoy your cooking you'll make better food, food that will make the people you love and cook for happy. And what is more important than that?

CHAPTER ONE

BREAKFAST & BRUNCH

Petit déjeuner et brunch

Egg, hollandaise & asparagus tartlets
Oeuf de poule Argenteuil

Serves four

200g asparagus
1 tbsp coarse salt
250ml hollandaise sauce
(see p.234)
4 baked savoury tartlet
shells (see shortcrust
pastry p.242)
1 tbsp white wine vinegar
4 free-range eggs
Salt and black pepper

Argenteuil, just outside Paris, is famous for its asparagus, which has a particularly wonderful flavour. When asparagus is in season, though, any kind will work well in this classic combination with poached eggs and hollandaise sauce, all encased in a crispy tart shell.

Take the asparagus and bend the stalk of each one until it snaps, then discard the woody ends. Peel the stalks if you think it necessary.

Bring a large pan of water to the boil and add the coarse salt. Add the asparagus and cook for 2 minutes. Drain the asparagus and refresh it in a bowl of ice-cold water to preserve the colour, then set it aside.

Cut off the top 7.5cm of each spear. Chop the remaining stems, mix them with half the hollandaise sauce and then divide them between the tartlet shells. Lay the asparagus spears over the top so the tips are showing. Preheat the grill.

Bring a pan of water to the boil and add the white wine vinegar. This helps set the white of the egg into a nice shape. Crack each egg into a bowl, start stirring the boiling water, then add the eggs and turn the heat down to a simmer. Poach the eggs for 3–4 minutes, not allowing the water to come back to the boil, until the whites look cooked, then remove the eggs and drain them on kitchen paper.

Top each tart with a poached egg and season with salt and pepper. Carefully spread the rest of the hollandaise over the eggs. Place the tartlets under the preheated grill until lightly browned, then serve immediately.

Prawn French toast with walnut & coriander pesto

Croque aux crevettes

450g peeled raw prawns
3 tbsp vegetable oil
3 free-range egg whites
3 free-range eggs
3 tbsp whole milk
Grating of nutmeg
8 slices of sourdough bread
Vegetable oil, for frying
1 tsp red chilli flakes,
    to serve (optional)
Salt and black pepper

Walnut & coriander pesto
60g walnuts
Big bunch of coriander
    (about 120g),
    roughly chopped
1 garlic clove,
    roughly chopped
1 tbsp grated Parmesan
1 green chilli roughly
    chopped, seeds removed
6 tbsp olive oil
Salt

A really special brunch dish, this is my French take on Chinese prawn toast. These are hearty sandwiches, so if you're serving them as part of a brunch buffet, just a half will be enough – unless you're not planning to eat again until the evening! The walnut and coriander pesto makes a nice change from the usual basil version. The recipe makes more than you need for the sandwiches, but the pesto keeps well in the fridge for a week and is delicious with pasta.

First, make the pesto. Put the walnuts, chopped coriander, garlic, Parmesan, chilli and olive oil into a blender and blitz to make a smooth mixture. Season with salt.

Put the prawns in a food processor with the oil and egg whites and season with salt and pepper. Blitz until smooth.

Beat the whole eggs with the milk in a bowl and season with salt, pepper and a grating of nutmeg, then set aside.

Divide the prawn mixture between 4 of the slices of bread, spreading it evenly, then top with the remaining slices. Cut the sandwiches in half, then dip each half into the egg mixture.

Pour some oil into a frying pan to a depth of about 1cm and heat. Shallow-fry the sandwiches, a few halves at a time, turning them until golden on all sides – this will take about 4 minutes in total. Drain the sandwiches on kitchen paper, then keep them warm in a low oven while you cook the rest.

Cut the sandwiches in half or into bite-sized pieces. Serve warm with the pesto and sprinkle a few chilli flakes on top if you want your sandwich to have a bit of a kick.

Potato & sweetcorn waffles with bacon crumb

Gaufres de pommes de terre et maïs doux

Serves four

Waffles
200g canned sweetcorn
250g flour
Caster sugar
3 free-range eggs, separated
200g whole milk
75g unsalted butter, melted
50g boiled new potatoes,
  cut into small dice
  (about 5mm)
2 tbsp vegetable oil
  and 2 tbsp butter
  (if frying the waffles)
Salt and black pepper

Bacon crumb
8 slices of streaky bacon

To serve (optional)
2 tbsp maple syrup

My family all love waffles and this savoury version brings all our favourite brunch flavours together. These are great drizzled with a little maple syrup or just as they are – I sometimes like to add an egg on top. You can make the waffle mixture the night before, ready to cook in the morning.

First make the bacon crumb. Heat a frying pan, add the bacon and fry until crispy, then drain it on kitchen paper. When the bacon is completely dry, chop it or crumble it with your fingers.

For the waffles, blitz 100g of the sweetcorn in a blender to make a smooth purée. Stir in the remaining 100g of sweetcorn.

Put the flour and a teaspoon of sugar in a bowl and season with salt and pepper. Add the egg yolks, milk and sweetcorn mixture, then whisk until smooth. Stir in the melted butter.

Whisk the egg whites until frothy, then add a tablespoon of sugar and continue to whisk until they form stiff peaks. Gently fold the egg whites into the sweetcorn mixture, then add the boiled potatoes and check the seasoning. Bake the waffles in a waffle maker until crispy and brown.

If you don't have a waffle maker, heat a small frying pan and add a little oil. Pour in a ladleful of the mixture and leave to set. Add some butter at the side of the waffle to brown it, then flip the waffle over and add more butter to brown the other side.

Serve the waffles topped with the crumbled bacon and with maple syrup, if using, on the side.

Potato rösti with onion & garlic
Crique Ardéchoise

2 large floury potatoes
1 onion, thinly sliced
2 garlic cloves, chopped
2 tbsp chopped parsley
2 tbsp vegetable oil
1 tbsp butter
Salt and black pepper

To serve
Chopped chives
Smoked salmon
Crème fraiche

This is a dish from the Ardèche –the region where I live when in France. It's a good alternative to hash browns and can also be served with roast meat, but my favourite is to serve it with smoked salmon. The key to success is to use good floury potatoes. The rösti, or criques, don't have to be neat but they should be nice and crispy.

Peel the potatoes, grate them on to a clean tea towel and squeeze out as much moisture as possible. Season with salt and pepper, then add the onion, garlic and parsley.

Heat the vegetable oil in a non-stick frying pan. Divide the potato mixture into 4 and shape into rounds, then add them to the frying pan.

Once the mixture has set, dot butter around the sides of the rösti. Once the butter has melted, flip the rösti over and add more butter at the sides. Continue to cook over a medium heat until golden and cooked through. If you prefer, you can cook one big rösti or crique and cut it into quarters.

Remove the rösti from the pan and drain on kitchen paper. Sprinkle with chopped chives and serve immediately with smoked salmon and dollops of crème fraiche.

'Pizza' with figs, goat cheese & ham
Petit pain aux figues et jambon cru

Serves four

Dough
7g sachet of fast-action
    dried yeast
90ml lukewarm water
25ml milk
250g bread flour,
    plus extra for dusting
1 tsp salt
½ tsp sugar
1 free-range egg, beaten
35g melted butter

Topping
1 free-range egg, beaten
2 large red onions,
    thinly sliced
3 garlic cloves, thinly sliced
6-8 ripe figs, thickly sliced
4 tbsp chestnut honey
150g soft goat cheese
    (Faisselle or goat curd)
Fresh lemon thyme sprigs
20g hard goat cheese
    (crottin or Pélardon)
Olive oil
Salt and black pepper

To serve
200g air-dried ham,
    such as Bayonne,
    Parma or Serrano

If you make the lovely rich brioche dough the night before, these don't take long to finish off in the morning. The tanginess of the red onion works perfectly with the sweetness of the figs, and the drizzle of honey on top adds a nice touch of indulgence. Add some Bayonne or other air-dried ham on the side for an ideal brunch.

First make the dough. Put the yeast in a bowl and pour in the lukewarm water and the milk. Mix well, then add the flour, salt, sugar, egg and melted butter. Knead the dough for 4–5 minutes on a floured surface until it is elastic, shiny and smooth. Put the dough back in the bowl, cover with a damp cloth and chill for 3–4 hours or overnight in the fridge. You can make the dough in a stand mixer if you have one.

Divide the dough into 4 balls. Place these on a floured surface, roll them out to about 5mm thick, then place them on a sheet of non-stick baking parchment. Brush the dough with beaten egg, then leave for 20 minutes to rise.

Preheat the oven to 240°C/Fan 220°C/Gas 9. Just before placing the 'pizzas' in the oven, spread the onions and garlic over the bases, dividing them equally, then add the sliced figs, honey, soft goat cheese and fresh thyme, again dividing them equally. Next, grate the hard goat cheese on top and drizzle with a little olive oil. Season with salt and pepper, then bake for about 20 minutes. Serve warm with the ham on the side.

Cheese & ham soufflés
Soufflés au fromage et jambon

Serves four

1 tbsp butter
1 tbsp plain flour
120ml milk
1 free-range egg yolk
Grating of nutmeg
100g grated cheese,
    a mix of Comté,
    Gruyère and Parmesan
8 free-range egg whites
100g good-quality cooked
    ham, chopped
Salt and black pepper

For the moulds
50g butter, melted
20g Parmesan, grated

These make a really impressive brunch dish for a special occasion – they will be greeted with gasps of delight! I like to add a little ham to my soufflés, but you can vary the surprise inside and use spicy sausage or smoked salmon instead, or vegetables such as spinach or broccoli. Delicious and easier than you think to make.

Preheat the oven to 200°C/Fan 180°C/Gas 6. You will need 4 large ramekins, about 10cm in diameter and 8cm high.

Brush the inside of each mould with melted butter and dust with grated Parmesan.

Melt the tablespoon of butter in a saucepan, add the flour and stir to make a thick paste. Add the milk and bring to the boil, stirring constantly. After about 5 minutes the sauce should have thickened. Remove the pan from the heat and leave the sauce to cool a little, then stir in the egg yolk. Season with salt, pepper and nutmeg, then add 65g of the cheese.

Whisk the egg whites with a little salt until stiff, then fold them into the sauce. Divide half the mixture between the ramekins, then add the chopped ham, dividing it equally. Then add the rest of the mixture and sprinkle the remaining cheese on top. Run your finger around the edge of each dish to prevent the soufflés from sticking.

Bake the soufflés in the preheated oven for 10–12 minutes, then serve immediately.

Omelette with anchovies
Omelette Provençale

8 free-range eggs
1 pinch of piment d'espelette
 or chilli flakes
1 tbsp tomato paste
12 salted anchovy fillets
1 tbsp oil
1 tbsp unsalted butter
1 tbsp chopped parsley
1 tbsp melted butter
Salt and black pepper

I'm very fond of anchovies and they add a wonderful salty flavour to this super-tasty breakfast omelette. Look for the best-quality anchovies you can find and go for salted ones, not those in vinegar. If you want to remove some of the saltiness, just rinse the anchovies in water before using. As always with omelettes, the secret of success here is to keep the texture slightly runny.

Crack the eggs into a bowl and beat them lightly with salt, pepper and the piment d'espelette or chilli flakes. Whisk in the tomato paste.

Roughly chop 8 of the anchovies and set the rest aside. Heat a large frying pan with a tablespoon of oil, then add the butter and the chopped anchovies.

Pour in the eggs and leave them for 10 seconds, then start to stir with a spatula. Add the chopped parsley. When the omelette is almost set, stop stirring and leave it to colour. Then tilt the pan and fold the omelette in half. The perfect omelette should be 'baveuse' – slightly runny and moist, not dry.

Arrange the whole anchovy fillets on top of the omelette and brush it with the melted butter. Cut the omelette into 4 wedges and serve at once.

Blue cheese sausage rolls
Roulés au fromage

375g ready-rolled puff pastry
Plain flour, for dusting
450g good-quality
    sausage meat
200g Bleu d'auvergne,
    Fourme d'ambert or
    Colston Bassett Stilton,
    rind removed, crumbled
50g chopped walnuts
1 egg, beaten
Salt and black pepper

Packed with sausage, blue cheese and walnuts, these are a real treat. They can be prepared the day before, ready to pop in the oven when you're ready to eat. It's important to get good sausage meat or just buy your favourite sausages and remove the skins. I'm a fan of blue cheese, but if you're not, use any strong-flavoured cheese instead.

Place the puff pastry on a floured work surface and roll it out as thinly as you can. Cut it in half lengthways into 2 strips of about 20cm wide.

Put the sausage meat and crumbled cheese into a bowl. Add the chopped walnuts and season, then mix with your hands until everything is well combined.

Divide the mixture in half, then form each piece into a sausage shape. Place one of these along a strip of pastry. Brush the edge of the pastry with a little beaten egg, then roll over the pastry so the seam is underneath and then press to seal. Repeat with the remaining sausage mixture and pastry.

Put the prepared rolls in the freezer to firm up for 15 minutes, as this makes them easier to cut. Preheat the oven to 220°C/Fan 200°C/Gas 7 and line a baking tray with baking paper.

Remove the rolls from the freezer and cut each roll into 6 pieces. Place them on the baking tray and brush with beaten egg. Bake for 15–20 minutes until puffed up and golden brown.

Venison turnovers
Petit pâté pantin

Makes six

375g ready-rolled puff pastry
Flour, for dusting
2 tbsp wholegrain mustard,
plus extra to serve
400g venison leg or shoulder
(ask your butcher to
mince it for you)
200g pork fat (ask your
butcher to mince it
for you)
1 tsp herbes de Provence
1 tsp piment d'espelette
or chilli flakes
2 juniper berries, crushed
1 free-range egg, beaten
Salt and black pepper

A traditional French version of a sausage roll, these are great to eat hot or cold at any time of day and are perfect for a savoury brunch. I remember making them as a young apprentice with different types of game, including partridge or pheasant, but venison is a favourite.

Place the puff pastry on a floured work surface and roll it out as thinly as you can. Cut it in half lengthways into 2 strips of about 20cm wide. Brush down one half of each strip with mustard.

Put the minced venison and pork fat in a bowl and season with the herbs, piment d'espelette or chilli flakes, crushed juniper berries, salt and black pepper. Divide the mixture between the 2 strips of pastry, spooning it over the mustard to a thickness of about 2.5cm.

Brush the uncovered side of each strip with beaten egg and fold it over the meat. Press the edges of the pastry together firmly so there is no air left in the roll, then go over them again with the tines of a fork.

Put the prepared rolls in the freezer to firm up for 15 minutes, as this makes them easier to cut. Preheat the oven to 200°C/ Fan 180°C/Gas 6 and line a baking tray with baking paper.

Remove the rolls from the freezer and slice each roll into 3 pieces. Place them on the baking tray and brush with beaten egg. Bake in the preheated oven for 25 minutes or until golden brown. Leave to cool for about 10 minutes, then serve with some more wholegrain mustard on the side.

Pancakes with honey & fresh berries

Crêpes au miel et fruits rouges

Makes twelve pancakes

Pancakes
5 free-range eggs
60g caster sugar
750ml buttermilk
½ tsp vanilla extract
500g self-raising flour
1 tbsp baking powder
1 tsp salt
100ml vegetable oil,
    plus extra for frying
2 tbsp butter

To serve
2 tbsp icing sugar (optional)
50g runny honey
1 punnet of raspberries
1 punnet of blackberries
1 punnet of blueberries

These American-style thick pancakes are a Sunday treat and are one of my grandson's favourite things. We make them together, then devour them warm from the pan with plenty of berries and honey. If you like, you can use gluten-free flour, which makes very light pancakes.

Mix the eggs, sugar, buttermilk and vanilla together in a bowl. Sift the flour into a separate bowl and stir in the baking powder and salt. Gradually add the dry ingredients to the wet, making sure there are no lumps, then gently stir in the 100ml of oil. Leave the batter to rest in the fridge for a couple of hours or, even better, overnight.

When you're ready to cook, heat a frying pan, 10–12cm in diameter, over a medium heat. Add a little oil, then a medium-sized ladleful of batter and swirl it around. (If you don't have a small enough pan, use more batter and make bigger pancakes.)

Allow the batter to set slightly, then dot some butter around the pancake. When it has turned golden brown, flip the pancake over and add some butter at the side again. Cook until the pancake is golden brown. Remove the pancake from the pan and keep it warm in a low oven while you cook the rest.

Serve the pancakes warm, sprinkled with a little icing sugar, if using, and drizzled with honey, with some fresh berries.

Apple turnovers
Chausson aux pommes

850g eating apples, peeled,
 cored and chopped
 (1kg unpeeled weight)
4 tbsp brown sugar
2 tbsp Calvados
500g block of all-butter
 puff pastry
Flour, for dusting
1 free-range egg, beaten

Syrup glaze
2 tbsp caster sugar
1 cinnamon stick
4 tbsp hot water

These little pastries are much loved by my wife, Gisèle. When we go to a patisserie, nine times out of ten she will buy a chausson — a lovely little parcel of buttery puff pastry filled with apple compote. They're good to eat at breakfast or any time of day. I use a mixture of apples, some tart and some sweet, for texture and flavour, and I do like to add the glaze for a nice finishing touch.

Put the apples, sugar and 2 tablespoons of water in a pan, cover with a lid and cook until the apples are soft. Remove the lid and stir well over a high heat until the liquid is almost gone. Remove from the heat and add the Calvados, then leave to cool. Put the apple compote in the fridge.

Roll out the pastry on a floured surface to a thickness of about 4mm. Cut out 12 discs about 10cm in diameter, re-rolling the trimmings as necessary. Put the discs in the fridge to chill.

Preheat the oven to 200°C/Fan 180°C/Gas 6. Roll the pastry discs into oval shapes. Place about 2 tablespoons of compote in the centre of each, brush the edges with beaten egg, then fold them over to make half-moon shapes.

Crimp the edges firmly to seal and prevent leakage, then, using the tip of a knife, press the edges together without cutting through the pastry. Brush the tops with beaten egg, place the parcels on a baking tray and bake for 20 minutes.

For the glaze, put the caster sugar and cinnamon in a pan with the hot water. Boil for about 5 minutes until the mixture has a syrupy consistency. When the pastries come out of the oven, brush them with the syrup and serve immediately.

Cinnamon rolls
Petit pains à la cannelle

Makes six rolls

Basic dough
250ml whole milk
1 medium free-range egg
80g light brown soft sugar
1 tsp ground cinnamon
½ tsp salt
7g sachet of fast-action
    dried yeast
450g strong white flour,
    plus extra for dusting
100g unsalted butter,
    softened
1 free-range egg, lightly
    beaten, for brushing
    the buns

Filling
50g unsalted butter, softened
80g dark brown soft sugar
2 tsp ground cinnamon
1 free-range egg,
    lightly beaten

Glaze
4 tbsp light brown soft sugar
2 tbsp hot water
1 tbsp golden caster sugar
1 tsp ground cinnamon

Cinnamon has a natural sweetness and is something we use a lot in French baking. The dough for these delicious rolls can be made in advance and kept in the fridge. Remove it half an hour before cooking.

For the dough, pour the milk into a small pan and warm it over a gentle heat. Remove the pan from the heat and allow the milk to cool slightly before using.

In a large bowl, whisk the egg with the sugar, cinnamon, salt, yeast and warm milk. Slowly mix in 300g of the flour, a little at a time. Add the rest of the flour and the 100g of softened butter, then bring the mixture together with your hands to form a soft, sticky dough. Knead until the dough does not stick to the bowl.

Turn the dough out on to a floured work surface, sprinkle with a little more flour and knead lightly until just smooth. Do not overwork the dough; it should only just hold together as a semi-smooth ball. Place the dough in a clean bowl, cover and leave at room temperature for an hour or until doubled in size.

Turn the risen dough out on to the floured work surface, sprinkle with a little more flour and roll it out into a large rectangle measuring about 30 x 40cm. Spread the 50g of butter over the dough and sprinkle with the dark brown sugar and cinnamon.

Line a couple of baking trays with baking paper. Gently roll the dough into a sausage shape, trim the ends neatly, then slice into 2.5cm rounds. Place the rounds on the baking trays and leave them to rise for 20 minutes – or if making the rolls in advance, put them in the fridge until ready to bake. Preheat the oven to 220°C/Fan 200°C/Gas 7. Brush the risen buns with beaten egg, then bake for 25 minutes. Transfer to a cooling rack.

To glaze, dissolve the light brown soft sugar in the hot water and brush this mixture lightly over the buns. Mix the tablespoon of caster sugar with the teaspoon of cinnamon and sprinkle over the top, then leave to cool.

CHAPTER TWO

QUICK LUNCHES

Repas sur le pouce

Omelette with mushrooms, parsley & sheep cheese

Omelette aux champignons, persil et fromage de brebis

Serves two

6 free-range eggs
100g wild mushrooms
    or button mushrooms,
    trimmed
Vegetable oil
1 tbsp finely chopped
    flatleaf parsley
½ garlic clove,
    finely chopped
2 tbsp butter
50g sheep cheese
    (Fleur de Maquis
    or Berkswell), grated
Salt and black pepper

Eggs are my idea of the perfect fast food – quick, nutritious and delicious. We often go foraging for mushrooms when we're in France and just a handful goes a long way in an omelette. My dad and my Uncle Michel used to have full-on arguments over omelettes. Uncle Michel liked his to have some colour, but Dad preferred no colour.

Beat the eggs in a bowl and season with salt and pepper.

Wipe the mushrooms and slice them into small pieces. Heat a little oil in a pan and fry the mushrooms, adding the parsley and garlic. Season and set aside.

Heat a 20cm omelette pan until very hot, then add a drop of oil and the butter. The butter should turn golden, but don't let it burn. Pour in the eggs and leave them for 10 seconds or so before mixing with a fork or spatula.

Once the omelette is setting but still a little underdone, add the mushrooms in the centre and sprinkle over the grated cheese. Tilt the pan and fold the omelette over the mushrooms.

Flip the omelette on to a warm plate and cut it in half to serve. It should be light and fluffy with a little colour.

Squash soup with roasted seeds
Velouté de courge

1 tbsp olive oil
750g squash, peeled
    and chopped
2 medium onions,
    thinly sliced
2 garlic cloves, chopped
Pinch of allspice
1 litre chicken stock
    or vegetable stock
50g pumpkin seeds
50g sunflower seeds
30g sesame seeds
Salt and black pepper

To serve
100ml crème fraiche
Pumpkin seed oil (optional)

Soups are a daily feature in France and I love this winter warmer. Caramelising the squash brings out its sweetness and I like to serve this topped with some crunchy roasted seeds to add texture as well as flavour. Filling and full of goodness.

Heat the oil in a large pan, add the squash and cook until it's nicely caramelised. Add the onions and garlic and cook until soft, then add the allspice. Pour in the stock and bring to the boil, then simmer for 20–30 minutes.

For the seeds, preheat the oven to 200°C/Fan 180°C/Gas 6. Put the seeds on a baking tray and roast them for 10 minutes until they're golden brown and crispy. Set aside.

Blend the soup in a food processor or with a stick blender, then, if you want a very smooth finish, pass the soup through a fine sieve. Taste and season with salt and pepper.

Serve the soup in bowls, topped with a dollop of crème fraiche and sprinkled with some of the roasted seeds. If you have some pumpkin seed oil, drizzle a few drops on top of the soup.

Fresh tomato soup

Velouté de tomate

Serves four to six

1 tbsp unsalted butter
1 onion, roughly chopped
3 garlic cloves,
    roughly chopped
800g ripe tomatoes, diced
¼ tsp cayenne pepper
    (optional)
¼ tsp piment d'espelette
    or chilli flakes
500ml vegetable stock
Salt and black pepper

Sourdough croutons
4-6 slices of
    sourdough bread
2 tbsp olive oil
3 garlic cloves, crushed

To serve
Crème fraiche
    or double cream

The key to success with this silky-smooth soup is to use really ripe tomatoes. The soup is flavoured with onion, garlic and a good kick of spice, so is warming both in heat and taste.

Melt the butter in a heavy-based pan over a medium heat and when the butter is foaming, add the onion and garlic. Cook for about 3 minutes, stirring occasionally, until the onion has turned translucent but not caramelised. Add the tomatoes, spices and stock, then stir and bring to a gentle boil. Cover the pan with a lid and leave the soup to cook gently for 20 minutes.

Using a blender, food mill or stick blender, purée the soup until smooth, then season with salt and pepper to taste. If you want a very smooth finish, pass the soup through a sieve.

For the croutons, preheat the oven to 220°C/Fan 200°C/Gas 7. Put the slices of bread on a baking tray lined with baking paper. Mix the olive oil with the garlic and drizzle it over the bread, then season with salt and pepper. Bake for about 10 minutes until golden and crisp.

Serve the soup hot, topped with dollops of crème fraiche or double cream and with the warm sourdough on the side.

Almond gazpacho with pickled peaches

Gaspacho aux amandes et pêches aigre-doux

Serves six

2 garlic cloves, peeled
200g whole almonds, peeled
200g sourdough bread,
    diced and crusts cut off
300g cucumber,
    peeled and diced
500ml almond milk
400ml olive oil
120ml sherry vinegar
1 green chilli, deseeded
    and chopped
Salt and black pepper

Pickled peaches
3 ripe yellow peaches,
    halved and stones removed
80g rice wine vinegar
60g caster sugar
8 coriander seeds
1 garlic clove, peeled
1 tarragon sprig
Pinch of salt

To garnish
Chopped herbs
Golden rapeseed oil (optional)

This white gazpacho is just as popular as the tomato versions in Spain and it's one of my favourite soups. It does need to marinate for a couple of hours but it keeps well in the fridge for several days so it's worth making a batch to enjoy ice cold for refreshing summer lunches.

For the pickled peaches, put the peach halves in a pan with all the other ingredients, add 60ml of water and bring to a simmer. Then take the pan off the heat and set aside to cool. Remove the peaches and slice them, then put them back in the liquid for about 2 hours. Drain them and place on kitchen paper.

If you don't have time to prepare the pickled peaches, you could just slice a few peaches and drizzle them with a little sherry vinegar, then serve them with the soup.

For the soup, bring a small pan of water to the boil, add the garlic and bring back to the boil. Remove and when the garlic cloves are cool enough to handle, remove the green centres.

Preheat the oven to 180°C/Fan 160°C/Gas 4. Spread the almonds out on a baking tray and bake for about 10 minutes to warm them and allow the flavour to develop. Don't let the almonds colour.

Place the garlic, almonds and all the rest of the ingredients for the soup in a large bowl. Add 500ml of water, then leave to marinate for a couple of hours. Tip everything into a blender and blitz to form a smooth texture, then pass through a fine sieve. Check the seasoning, then leave to chill in the fridge.

Serve the chilled gazpacho in bowls and add some peaches. Garnish with chopped herbs and drizzle each serving with golden rapeseed oil, if using.

Watercress soup with poached egg & black pudding

Velouté de cresson, œuf poché et boudin noir

Serves four

50g butter
Olive oil
2 shallots, thinly sliced
300g floury potatoes,
    cut into small chunks
1 litre white chicken stock
    or vegetable stock
400g watercress
2 tbsp chopped wild garlic
    (when in season or
    use chives)
200g black pudding, sliced
1 tbsp vinegar
4 free-range eggs
4 wild garlic flowers (when
    in season), to garnish
Salt and black pepper

There was a watercress soup on the original Gavroche menu back in 1967 and it is still much loved by my family. Watercress has a lovely peppery flavour and the addition of a poached egg and black pudding makes this soup into a really satisfying meal.

Melt the butter in a saucepan with a little splash of olive oil. Add the shallots, season with salt and sauté until soft.

Add the potatoes and stock, then continue to cook for about 15 minutes until the potatoes are soft. Add the watercress and wild garlic or chives and cook for 2 minutes, then transfer to a blender and blitz until smooth.

The soup will be a beautiful bright green. If you're preparing the soup in advance, pour it into a bowl set over a bowl of iced water. This will cool the soup quickly, so it retains its fresh green colour.

When you're nearly ready to eat, heat 2 tablespoons of oil in a frying pan, add the black pudding and fry for 4–6 minutes until golden brown. Drain it on kitchen paper.

To poach the eggs, bring a pan of water to the boil and add the vinegar. Crack the eggs into separate bowls. Swirl the water in the pan with a spoon, gently add the eggs and turn the heat down to a simmer. Poach the eggs for 4–5 minutes or until cooked but with soft yolks. Carefully remove the eggs with a slotted spoon and drain them on kitchen paper.

To serve, put some black pudding at the bottom of each bowl and place a poached egg on top of it. Reheat the soup, if you've made it in advance, and pour it around the black pudding and egg. Drizzle with a little olive oil and garnish with wild garlic flowers, if using.

Sweetcorn soup

Crème Caroline

Serves four

2 tbsp unsalted butter
½ onion, finely diced
350g tinned sweetcorn,
    drained and rinsed
800ml milk
Grating of nutmeg
Salt and black pepper

To serve
4 tsp crème fraiche
A few chives,
    finely chopped
Pinch of paprika
Cornbread (see p.241)
    or crusty bread

This is a really quick and easy soup as it's made with tinned sweetcorn, which is already cooked and super-sweet. A little pinch of nutmeg really lifts the flavour. I like to have this with cornbread (see page 241), but if you don't have time to make that, serve with some slices of good crusty bread.

Melt the butter in a pan, add the onion and sweat until soft, stirring from time to time. Do not allow the onion to colour. Add the well-drained sweetcorn and stir for a few minutes, then add the milk and nutmeg. Bring to a simmer and cook for 15 minutes.

Blitz the soup in a food processor or with a stick blender, then pass it through a fine sieve. Season to taste. The soup can be made a few days before, then reheated or served cold.

Garnish the soup with crème fraiche and chives and sprinkle with a little paprika. Serve with cornbread or crusty bread.

Dandelion salad with potatoes & bacon with quince vinaigrette

Salade de pissenlit aux pommes de terre, lardons et vinaigrette aux coings

Serves four

200g small new
  potatoes, unpeeled
300g small wild
  dandelion leaves
  (or frisée or escarole)
1 tbsp vegetable oil
200g smoked streaky bacon,
  cut into large lardons
1 onion, finely chopped
Salt and black pepper

Quince vinaigrette
5 tbsp olive oil
2 tbsp quince vinegar
  (or cider vinegar)
1 tbsp quince paste
  (membrillo), chopped
1 shallot, finely chopped
2 tsp Dijon mustard
Salt and black pepper

This is a play on the traditional salade lyonnaise. The saltiness of the bacon works beautifully with the sweetness of the quince in the dressing and the bitterness of the salad leaves – quince paste is available in many supermarkets and delis. If you're using wild dandelion leaves, be sure to pick them from unpolluted areas and give them a really good wash. If your potatoes are not very small and new, peel them after boiling and slice them thickly. You can also use leftover potatoes.

For the quince vinaigrette, mix all the ingredients together and set aside.

Put the potatoes in a pan of cold water, add salt and cook for about 20 minutes, until you can insert the point of a knife without meeting any resistance. Drain and leave them to cool.

Wash and dry the leaves and place them in a large salad bowl. If using dandelion leaves, wash them extra carefully in several changes of cold water, dry well and discard any larger leaves.

Heat the oil in a frying pan, add the bacon lardons and cook gently until crisp. Tip the lardons and their hot fat into a dish and set aside.

In the same pan, without wiping it out, cook the onion for one minute over a medium heat, stirring with a spatula. Pour in the vinaigrette, let it bubble, then add the well-drained potatoes. Roll them in the mixture for one minute, then add the lardons and fat. Pour the contents of the pan over the leaves. Season with salt and pepper, toss the salad and serve immediately.

Courgette salad with olives
Salade de courgettes et olives

500g mixed courgettes
(baby, green,
round, yellow)
2 medium shallots,
finely sliced
1 tbsp floral honey
Juice of 1 lemon and
zest of ½ lemon
4 tbsp good-quality
extra virgin olive oil
80g black olives, pitted
and roughly chopped
100g sundried tomatoes
in oil, sliced
1 tbsp chopped
flatleaf parsley
1 tbsp chopped chives
100g rocket leaves
Salt and black pepper

Courgette flowers (optional)
8 courgette flowers
1 litre vegetable oil,
for frying
2 tbsp cornflour

We don't always think of eating courgettes raw but they are delicious, particularly if you can find small ones, which are sweeter and have fewer seeds than the large ones. Mix different varieties if possible to get a range of flavour, texture and colour. I like to add the courgette flowers but if you can't get them, don't worry – the salad will still be good.

Using a mandolin or a sharp knife, cut the courgettes into a variety of shapes, such as thin slices, matchsticks, ribbons and dice. Put them in a serving bowl, add the shallots and season with salt and pepper.

Mix the honey with the lemon juice and zest, add the olive oil, then pour this dressing on to the courgettes.

Add the olives, sundried tomatoes and herbs, taste and season again if needed. Sprinkle some rocket leaves on top and serve.

If using the courgette flowers, open them carefully and remove the stamens which can be very bitter. Add the oil to a large pan and heat it until a square of bread browns in seconds. Dust the flowers with cornflour and deep-fry them for 2 minutes until crisp. Remove and drain on kitchen paper, then season with a little salt. Serve with the salad.

Asparagus, tomato & artichoke salad with grilled bread

Salade d'asperges, tomates et artichauts et son pain grillé

Serves two

2 slices of sourdough bread
Mild olive oil
1 small onion, diced
1 garlic clove, finely chopped
50ml dry white wine
Juice of ½ lemon
4 anchovies, chopped
  (optional)
125ml vegetable stock
300g thin asparagus spears
6 artichoke hearts,
  from a jar or deli pack
100g cherry tomatoes, halved
8 quails' eggs, boiled
  and peeled
3 tbsp fresh chives,
  basil and fresh mint,
  roughly chopped
Salt and black pepper

I like making warm salads for lunch and this recipe uses some store cupboard ingredients, such as artichoke hearts and anchovies. Lots of colour, lots of flavour – it's a joy to eat. The quails' eggs add a special touch but if you prefer, just top the salad with a poached hen's egg instead. If you do use quails' eggs, soak them in a strong vinegar solution for about three minutes once cooked. This softens the shells and makes the eggs easier to peel.

Preheat the oven to 220°C/Fan 200°C/Gas 7. Put the slices of sourdough on a baking tray, drizzle them with oil and season with salt and pepper. Bake for 5–10 minutes until crunchy.

Place a sauté pan over a high heat. Add 2 tablespoons of olive oil and sauté the onion and garlic for a couple of minutes. Then add the wine and lemon juice, bring to the boil and simmer for 2–3 minutes. Add the anchovies, if using, and pour in the stock. Bring to a simmer, then reduce the heat and simmer gently for 3–4 minutes.

Add the asparagus and artichoke hearts, stir gently and cook for 2–3 minutes. Sprinkle in the tomatoes and cook for 1–2 minutes or until they've softened and released a little of their juices. Add the quails' eggs to gently warm through for a couple of minutes, then remove the pan from the heat and tip the contents into a serving dish.

Drizzle the salad with a little olive oil, sprinkle with the chopped herbs and serve warm with the sourdough bread.

Melon salad with mint & aged balsamic vinegar

Salade de melon à la menthe et vieux vinaigre balsamique

Serves two

1 ripe Charentais melon
Juice of ½ lemon
1 tsp pink peppercorns,
    crushed
Handful of fresh mint, leaves
    picked and finely chopped
20ml extra virgin olive oil
20ml aged balsamic or
    regular balsamic vinegar
Salt

To serve
Charcuterie or goat cheese

The Provençal town of Cavaillon is famed for its melons. Indeed, it calls itself the melon capital of the world, such is the sweetness and flavour of the fruit grown there. Happily, these Charentais melons are readily available elsewhere – although they might not be quite as good without the Provençal soil and sun – or you can use other varieties. Just make sure your melon is sweet and ripe. The addition of pink peppercorns brings a spicy tang to the salad, but if you don't have any you could use green or Szechuan peppercorns. The salad is delicious on its own, but also goes well with some charcuterie or goat cheese.

Cut the melon in half, slice the flesh into chunks and put them in a bowl. Discard the seeds. Drizzle the melon with the lemon juice and sprinkle over the pink peppercorns and chopped mint.

Add the olive oil and balsamic vinegar, sprinkle with a little salt, then give everything a good stir and leave the flavours to infuse for a while.

This is best served at room temperature for the maximum flavour. Just before serving, stir well and check the seasoning.

Heritage tomato salad with anchovies, olives & croutons

Salade de tomates aux anchois, olives et croûtons

Serves four

600g heritage tomatoes
(plum, yellow pear, beef,
brandywine, green zebra,
sungold, kumato), cut into
different shapes
200g cherry tomatoes
on the vine, halved
8 tbsp extra virgin olive oil
4 tbsp white balsamic vinegar
1 red onion, finely sliced
Handful of fresh basil
leaves, torn
2 fresh oregano sprigs
100g pitted black olives
2 tbsp butter
4 slices of sourdough
bread, cut into cubes
16 salted anchovies (optional)
Salt and black pepper

To garnish
Fresh basil and oregano

To serve (optional)
Fresh cheese, such as
mozzarella, Faisselle
or goat curd

This salad sings summer to me. By using heritage tomatoes, you get a wonderful range of colours and textures and of course, taste. Tomatoes work beautifully with salty anchovies and olives, and the addition of some fresh cheese makes this into a complete meal. Never, ever keep your tomatoes in the fridge. They should always be served at room temperature for the best flavour.

Put all the tomatoes in a salad bowl, sprinkle with salt and pepper and leave to marinate for about 5 minutes. Add the oil and vinegar and leave for a further 5 minutes, then add the sliced onion, chopped herbs and olives.

Heat a frying pan, add the butter and fry the cubes of bread until golden brown. Drain them on kitchen paper, season with salt and leave to cool.

Sprinkle the croutons on top of the tomatoes and garnish with the anchovies, if using. Garnish with more herbs before serving with fresh cheese, if using.

Smoked fish salad
Salade de poissons fumés

Serves four

500g smoked fish (mackerel,
   trout, salmon or halibut)

Salad
2 Little Gem lettuces
4 heads of red chicory

Sauce verte
5g each of dill, chives,
   parsley, tarragon
   and basil leaves
200ml vegetable oil
1 tbsp Dijon mustard
2 free-range egg yolks
1 tbsp tarragon vinegar
1 lemon, cut into wedges
Salt and black pepper

There's plenty of good smoked fish available now in fishmongers and supermarkets. I like to mix different types, such as trout, mackerel, salmon and halibut, for this quick, tasty salad. The sauce verte recipe will make more than you need but it keeps in the fridge for several days.

For the sauce verte, put the herbs in a food processor or blender with the oil and blend until the mixture is bright green.

Tip this mixture out of the blender, wash the blender, then add the mustard, egg yolks and season with salt and pepper. Blend, then start adding the herb oil a little at a time to make a sauce with a mayonnaise-like consistency. If it becomes too thick, add a little water.

Separate the lettuce and heads of chicory into leaves. Serve the smoked fish, broken into pieces, over the salad leaves, with lemon wedges and the sauce verte on the side.

Roast cod cheeks with watercress salad
Joues de morue rôties et salade de cresson

Serves two

1 tbsp white wine vinegar
5 tbsp olive oil
250g cod cheeks
80g watercress,
 washed and dried
4 medium tomatoes, peeled,
 deseeded and diced
60g green olives, pitted
 and sliced lengthwise
 into 3mm slivers
Salt and black pepper

Cod cheeks are delicious little nuggets of fish and are usually cheaper than cod fillet. They cook quickly and partner well with the tomatoes, olives and peppery watercress in this recipe. You could also make this dish with monkfish or skate cheeks.

Add the vinegar to a bowl and season with 2 pinches of salt and a grinding of pepper. Slowly add 3 tablespoons of the olive oil, a little at a time, whisking constantly. Put this dressing in the fridge while you cook the fish.

Season the cheeks on both sides. Heat the remaining olive oil in a frying pan and brown the cheeks on both sides over a high heat. This will take 3–5 minutes, depending on the thickness of the cheeks. They should stay soft – be careful not to overcook them or they will be tough. Remove them from the pan.

Toss the watercress with the dressing, then add the tomatoes and olives and mix well. Arrange the salad on a dish, then top with the warm cod cheeks and serve.

Grilled marinated mackerel
Maquereau mariné et grillé

Serves two

4 large fillets of mackerel
Mixed salad leaves

Marinade
1 tbsp finely chopped basil
1 tsp finely chopped
    root ginger
1 garlic clove, crushed
    to a purée
2–3 tbsp olive oil
Zest and juice of ½ lemon
1 tsp chilli flakes

Dressing
2 tbsp olive oil
Juice of ½ lemon
½ tbsp clear honey
½ fresh red chilli, chopped
Salt and black pepper

Mackerel is cheap to buy, sustainable and delicious to eat, particularly when it's really fresh. Ask your fishmonger to pin bone the fish for you and this is then a super-quick meal to put together. The brief marinade adds flavour and the salad leaves with the spicy, tangy dressing are a perfect accompaniment to the oily fish.

Mix the marinade ingredients together in a bowl, add the fish and leave it to marinate for 10–20 minutes.

Meanwhile, whisk the dressing ingredients together and preheat your grill to 250°C.

Remove the mackerel fillets from the marinade, place them skin-side up under the hot grill and baste a few times with the marinade. Cook for 4–5 minutes until just charred. Dress the salad leaves and serve with the fish.

CHAPTER THREE

SIMPLE SUPPERS FOR TWO

Simples dîners pour deux

Truffade with bitter leaf salad
Truffade Auvergnate

Serves two

3 tbsp duck fat
100g bacon lardons
400g potatoes, cut into
    thin slices (about 3mm)
200g good melting cheese,
    such as Gruyère, Cantal,
    Comté or Fontina, sliced
2 garlic cloves,
    finely chopped
Salt and black pepper

Bitter leaf salad
200g frisée
1 head of white chicory
1 head of red chicory

Vinaigrette
5 tbsp olive oil
2 tbsp white wine vinegar
1 tsp Dijon mustard
½ shallot, finely chopped
1 garlic clove, finely chopped
1 tbsp finely chopped parsley
1 tbsp finely chopped chives

This is a warming, hearty dish, similar to tartiflette – just the thing on a cold winter's day. You do need a good-quality melting cheese and be sure to keep the bacon lardons quite chunky and the potatoes thinly sliced for the best results. The bitter leaf salad helps to cut through the richness of the cheese and the duck fat. Last but not least, have a glass of good strong red wine to wash it all down!

For the salad, wash and dry the frisée and chicory and cut them into small pieces. Mix the dressing ingredients together in a jug and season to taste.

For the truffade, heat the duck fat in a large non-stick frying pan, add the bacon lardons and fry until golden. Add the potato slices and season with salt and pepper to taste. Cook for about 30 minutes over a medium heat, stirring from time to time, until tender and browned.

Turn the heat down to low and arrange the slices of cheese on top of the potatoes. Cook for a few minutes until the cheese has melted – covering the pan with a lid speeds up this process. Add the garlic, then take the pan off the heat and stir, turning everything over with a spatula.

Using the spatula, pull the potatoes and cheese away from the edge of the pan, then shake the pan back and forth to make sure the entire mass is detached from the base of the pan. Flip the truffade like a pancake, then cook it for a minute or so longer over a low heat.

If you don't feel confident about flipping the truffade, place a plate over the pan and turn the truffade on to the plate. Then slide it back into the pan to cook the other side for a minute or so. Serve immediately with the salad and some bread.

Creamy onion tagliatelle
Tagliatelles aux oignons et crème

1 tbsp unsalted butter
2 medium onions,
    finely chopped
1 garlic clove, finely chopped
1 free-range egg yolk
100g blue cheese, crumbled,
    plus extra to garnish
60ml double cream
1 tbsp cognac
300g fresh tagliatelle or
    200g dried tagliatelle
Salt and black pepper

Pasta is a regular supper in our family and this bowlful of creamy deliciousness is a great favourite. The onions are cooked down until they are really soft and sweet and they marry perfectly with the tanginess of the blue cheese.

Melt the butter in a large pan over a medium-low heat. Add the chopped onions and garlic and toss them in the butter, then cook for 4–5 minutes until the onions begin to soften. Turn the heat down to low and continue to cook the onions until they are very soft and a deep golden-brown colour, stirring them every 4 or 5 minutes. This should take 20–25 minutes.

Meanwhile, whisk the egg yolk, blue cheese and cream in a bowl and season with salt and black pepper. Set aside.

Bring a large saucepan of water to the boil and season it with 2 tablespoons of salt.

When the onions are caramelised, add the cognac. Turn the heat up to medium, then simmer until the cognac has reduced. Take the pan off the heat and set aside.

As soon as you've added the cognac to the onions, drop the pasta into the pan of boiling water. Cook the pasta until it's al dente, then drain it and add it to the onions. Turn the heat down to medium-low and toss the pasta with the onions. Season with salt and pepper.

Add the egg mixture to the pasta and onions. Using tongs, keep tossing the pasta with the sauce until the blue cheese has melted. Remove from heat, season to taste with salt and pepper, then serve immediately.

Tagliatelle with pistou
Tagliatelles au pistou

2 bunches of basil,
    leaves only
4 garlic cloves,
    finely chopped
200ml olive oil
300g fresh tagliatelle or
    200g dried tagliatelle
50g firm goat cheese or
    sheep cheese (such as
    crottin or Berkswell)
Salt and black pepper

Pistou is the French version of Italian pesto, made with just basil, garlic and olive oil – no cheese or nuts – and perfect for a super-quick pasta supper. This pistou recipe makes more than you need for two, but it keeps well in the fridge for another time.

For the pistou, purée the basil, garlic and olive oil in a blender and season with salt and pepper.

Bring a pan of water to the boil and add 2 tablespoons of salt. Cook the pasta until al dente, then drain. Tip the pasta back into the pan, add spoonfuls of pistou to taste, then toss well.

Reheat the pistou and pasta for about 2 minutes over a low heat and season again. Toss well, then serve in bowls, topped with some thin slices of firm goat or sheep cheese.

Linguine with olives, artichokes, sundried tomatoes & herbs

Linguine aux olives, artichauts, tomates séchées et herbes fraîches

Serves two

2 tbsp extra virgin olive oil
1 garlic clove, finely chopped
1 shallot, finely chopped
200g chopped tomatoes,
    from a can
8 sundried tomatoes, from
    a jar, roughly chopped
8 cooked artichokes,
    from a jar or deli pack,
    roughly chopped
2 pinches of dried chilli flakes
1 tbsp salted capers, rinsed
12 black olives, pitted
250g fresh linguine
    or 180g dried linguine
Salt and black pepper

To serve
Handful of basil leaves, torn
60g Parmesan, grated

Using mostly store cupboard ingredients, this is another speedy pasta supper that we often enjoy. I like the intense flavours of the artichokes, olives and sundried tomatoes, all topped off with some grated Parmesan or other mature cheese.

Heat the olive oil in a frying pan. Add the garlic and shallot and stir for about 2 minutes over a medium heat. Add the chopped tomatoes and a pinch of salt, then cook over a high heat for 2–3 minutes, stirring often.

Add the chopped sundried tomatoes and artichokes and season with the chilli flakes, salt and pepper. Turn the heat down low and cook for 2–3 minutes, then stir in the capers and olives and cook for another minute.

Bring a pan of water to the boil and add 2 tablespoons of salt. Cook the pasta until al dente, then drain, reserving some of the cooking water. Add the pasta to the sauce and heat through, adding 3 ladlefuls of the cooking water to moisten the sauce. Season to taste.

Divide the pasta between 2 plates and scatter over the basil leaves. Serve with grated Parmesan.

Braised chicory in ham with béchamel sauce

Gratin d'endives au jambon

4 large heads of chicory
20g butter, for greasing
4 slices of cooked ham
   (Torchon works well)
100g Gruyère, grated
Salt and black pepper

Béchamel sauce
30g unsalted butter
30g plain flour
500ml whole milk
Pinch of cayenne pepper
Grating of nutmeg
1 tbsp crème fraiche
Salt and black pepper

This is a classic, a dish I was brought up on like most French children, especially in northern France. Blanching the chicory is important to remove some of the bitterness and be sure to squeeze out as much liquid from them as you can. The dish can be prepared in advance, ready to pop into the oven half an hour before you want to eat.

Bring a pan of salted water to the boil, add the heads of chicory and cook them for about 15 minutes, until tender. Remove them from the water and drain them on kitchen paper, then press out any excess liquid.

Take a gratin dish measuring about 26 x 30cm and 5cm deep or which has a capacity of about 2.5 litres and grease it with butter. Wrap each head of chicory in a slice of ham and place them in the dish. Preheat the oven to 180°C/Fan 160°C/Gas 4.

To make the sauce, melt the butter in a pan, then whisk in the flour, making sure there are no lumps. Stir for 2 or 3 minutes over a low heat, then add the milk and whisk to make a smooth sauce. Bring to a bubble, then turn the heat down to a simmer and cook for up to 10 minutes, stirring frequently. Season to taste with cayenne, nutmeg, salt and pepper, then stir in the crème fraiche.

Pour the hot sauce over the chicory and sprinkle the grated Gruyère on top. Bake for 20–30 minutes until golden brown with a lovely crust. Remove and leave the dish to rest for a few minutes as it will be piping hot, then serve.

Poached cod with orange & vermouth

Morue pochée à l'orange et au vermouth

Serves two

1 orange
2 x 200g cod fillets
    (or other white fish,
    such as hake or pollock)
Sea salt
1 tbsp olive oil
150ml dry vermouth
½ shallot, finely chopped
Chopped herbs (fennel,
    chives, parsley or basil)
40g crème fraiche
Black pepper

Garnish
1 tbsp olive oil
½ shallot, finely chopped
1 garlic clove, finely chopped
Knob of butter
100g baby spinach
40g samphire
    (if not available,
    use extra spinach)
Salt and black pepper

Gently poaching fish like this is a sure-fire way of keeping it beautifully moist. The orange works perfectly with the fish, and using vermouth instead of white wine adds extra flavour to the sauce. You can use other white fish instead of cod, if you prefer.

Wash the orange well, zest it and set the zest aside. Peel the orange and remove the segments over a bowl to catch any juice (see page 86 for guidance on how to do this). Squeeze the peel and membrane over the bowl to extract any remaining juice.

Generously sprinkle the fish with sea salt and the orange zest, then leave it to cure for 15 minutes. Rinse off the salt and pat the fish dry with kitchen paper.

Put the oil, vermouth and shallot in a frying pan with a lid and season with pepper. Bring to a simmer, then add the orange juice and bring to the boil. Gently add the fish, cover the pan with the lid and leave to cook for about one minute or so, depending on the thickness of the fillets. Take the pan off the heat and set it aside with the lid on for 5 minutes. The fish should be perfectly cooked.

Meanwhile, for the garnish, heat the oil in a separate pan and add the shallot, garlic and butter. Cook for 2 minutes, then add the spinach and cook until wilted. Add the samphire – or extra spinach – and season with salt and black pepper.

Remove the cod fillets from the pan and place them on warm plates. Add the chopped herbs and orange segments to the fish cooking juices in the pan and whisk in the crème fraiche. Bring the sauce back to the boil and pour it over the fish. Serve with the spinach and samphire, plus some new potatoes if you like.

Barbecued sea bass with rouille
Loup de mer grillé, sauce rouille

Serves two

2 fennel bulbs
1 sea bass (about 600g),
    gutted and cleaned
4 bay leaves
Extra virgin olive oil,
    to drizzle
1 lemon, cut in half
20 asparagus spears
    (a mixture of green
    and white)
Sea salt and black pepper

Rouille
100g cooked potato
3 hard-boiled free-range
    egg yolks
2 new-season's garlic
    cloves, peeled
Pinch of piment d'espelette
    or chilli flakes
2 pinches of saffron
4 good-quality salted
    anchovies
Juice of ½ lemon
1 tsp tomato paste
100ml olive oil
Salt

*Sea bass is perfect for barbecuing but can also be cooked on a griddle.
If cooking on the barbecue, a fish cage makes turning the fish much easier.*

For the rouille, peel the cooked potato and place the flesh in a blender. Add the egg yolks, garlic, piment d'espelette or chilli flakes, saffron, anchovies, lemon juice and tomato paste. Then add 75ml of the olive oil and blend until smooth. Taste for seasoning, then add the remaining oil and blend again. If the sauce splits, add a splash of water.

Heat the barbecue. Thinly slice one of the fennel bulbs and cut the other one into quarters, removing the hard core.

Make sure the fish is nicely cleaned and make a few slashes with a sharp knife through the skin. Sprinkle each side of the fish with sea salt and pepper, then sprinkle sea salt into the cavity and add the slices of fennel and the bay leaves. Drizzle both sides with a little oil and place the fish into a fish cage if you have one. Place the fish on to the barbecue and cook for about 5–8 minutes on the first side. Turn the fish and cook for another 5 minutes on the other side.

Drizzle the fennel quarters and lemon halves with a little olive oil and season with salt and pepper. Pop the fennel and lemon halves on to the barbecue and cook the fennel for 3–4 minutes on each side and the lemon until charred.

Next, place the asparagus spears on the barbecue – they will only take 2 minutes or so, depending on the heat. When the asparagus is cooked, remove it from the barbecue and place it on a serving dish with the fennel. Remove the fish and serve it on top of the vegetables, along with the charred lemons. Serve the rouille on the side.

If you don't have a barbecue, you can cook the fish on a griddle pan on the hob. The method is the same, but the fish will need to cook for about 10 minutes longer.

Cod & vegetable parcels
Cabillaud en papillote

Serves two

150g new potatoes,
   cooked and sliced
1 fennel bulb, thinly sliced
100g baby plum
   tomatoes, halved
½ lemon, cut into wedges
1 tbsp olive oil
50ml dry white wine
1 pinch of piment d'espelette
   or chilli flakes
1 thyme sprig
1 rosemary sprig
50g samphire
2 x 200g cod fillets
   or other white fish
20g pitted black olives,
   halved
Salt and black pepper

This is a simple dish with something of a wow factor – you bring the parcels to the table, open them up and inhale the lovely aromas of the fish and vegetables. The recipe works well with other white fish, such as hake or pollock, and you can use baby spinach or other greens when samphire is out of season. Prepare these in advance and then pop them in the oven when almost ready to eat.

Place the sliced potatoes, fennel, tomatoes and lemon wedges in a bowl. Drizzle them with olive oil, splash over a little of the wine and season with salt, pepper and piment d'espelette or chilli flakes. Heat a frying pan, then add the potato mixture. Cook over a gentle heat, stirring regularly, until everything is slightly coloured and tender.

Preheat the oven to 200°C/Fan 180°C/Gas 6. Cut 2 squares of greaseproof paper or foil, measuring about 40 x 40cm.

Divide the vegetables and the herbs between the squares of paper or foil and drizzle with a little oil. Add some samphire to each one, then a piece of fish, a few olives and the remaining wine. Scrunch the edges of the paper or foil together to form 2 parcels and place them on a baking tray. Bake for 20 minutes or until the fish is cooked through – the exact time will depend on the thickness of the fillets.

Serve the fish with some crusty sourdough for mopping up the tasty cooking juices.

Mussels Provençal
Moules à la provençale

1kg mussels
1 tbsp olive oil, plus
    extra to drizzle
1 onion, chopped
1 garlic clove, chopped
80g saucisson sec, diced
    (or an end piece of
    salami or dried ham)
150ml dry white wine
300g tomatoes, peeled,
    deseeded and chopped
1 roasted red pepper,
    from a jar, diced
Large handful of flatleaf
    parsley, finely chopped
12 black olives, pitted
Salt and black pepper

To serve
Crusty bread

This is a Provençal take on moules marinière, using dried sausage or salami to add a richer flavour. I also add roasted peppers, using the ones from a jar to save time. Easy, quick and good to eat.

Wash the mussels and scrape off the beards and any barnacles. Discard any mussels that don't close when they're tapped.

Heat a large pan and add the olive oil. When it's hot, add the onion, garlic and saucisson sec and sauté for a few minutes. Next, add the mussels and wine, cover the pan and cook for 5 minutes or until the mussels have opened. Discard any that don't open.

Drain the mussels, onion and saucisson in a colander set over a bowl and set aside. Pour the cooking liquid back into the pan, bring to the boil and reduce for 5 minutes. Add the tomatoes and red pepper, then season and simmer again until the sauce has thickened slightly.

Pick the flesh from most of the mussels, leaving some in the shell to use as a garnish. Place the mussels, onion and saucisson back in the sauce, then reheat gently. Sprinkle with chopped parsley and add the olives.

Ladle into big bowls and drizzle with a little extra virgin olive oil. Serve with some crusty bread.

Tagliolini with seafood, pastis & crème fraiche

Tagliolini aux fruits de mer, pastis et crème fraîche

Serves two

400g clams
500g mussels
2 tbsp olive oil
1 shallot, chopped
1 tsp fennel seeds
2 garlic cloves, chopped
50ml pastis
150g shelled raw prawns
4 tbsp crème fraiche
300g fresh tagliolini
   or 180g dried tagliolini
   or tagliatelle
Handful of herbs
   (parsley, chives, chervil),
   finely chopped
Juice of 1 lemon
Salt and black pepper

I love seafood, and pasta and shellfish are always a great combination. Keep this simple with mussels and clams or if you want to go to town, use other shellfish, such as razor clams or cockles, when they're in season. The fennel seeds and pastis bring that lovely aniseed flavour that works so well with seafood.

Wash the clams and mussels well in cold water and discard any that are broken or that don't close when tapped. Remove any beards from the mussels.

Heat the olive oil in a large pan, add the shallot, fennel seeds and garlic and sweat until they start to colour. Add the clams, then the mussels. Pour in the pastis, cover the pan and cook for 5–7 minutes until all the shells have opened. Take care not to overcook the shellfish.

Tip everything into a colander placed over a bowl, then pass the cooking liquid through a fine sieve or a strainer lined with muslin. Pick the flesh from the mussels and clams, leaving a few in the shell to use as a garnish. Tip the cooking liquor back into the pan, bring it to the boil and boil for 5 minutes. Add the prawns and crème fraiche, then, when the prawns have turned pink, add the picked mussels and clams.

Bring a pan of water to the boil and add 2 tablespoons of salt. Cook the pasta until al dente, then drain. Add the drained pasta to the pan of shellfish and stir well. Add the chopped herbs and garnish with some mussels and clams in shells. Season with lemon juice, salt and pepper, then serve at once.

Green asparagus with Comté crisps & wild mushrooms

Asperges vertes aux champignons et Comté

Serves two

60g Comté cheese, grated
16 large green
   asparagus spears
1 tbsp coarse salt
25g butter
200g girolles or a mixture
   of wild mushrooms,
   cleaned and sliced
   or left whole if small
1 bunch of chives,
   finely chopped
Juice of 1 lemon
100g rocket leaves
Salt and black pepper

When asparagus is in season I like to enjoy it as often as possible in dishes like this simple recipe for a light supper. If you can't find wild mushrooms, cultivated are fine and the crisp cheese on top makes a good contrast in flavour and texture.

For the Comté crisps, heat a non-stick frying pan and sprinkle the grated cheese over the base. Let it melt and when it's slightly brown, remove with a palette knife and set aside to cool down. Once the cheese is cool, break it into pieces.

Snap off the woody base of each asparagus spear and peel the stems if you think it necessary. Prepare a bowl of iced water.

Bring a large pan of water to the boil and add the coarse salt. Add the asparagus, cook for 2 minutes until it's tender and the point of a knife goes into a stem easily. Drain the asparagus, then put it in a bowl of iced water so it retains its colour. Drain the asparagus when cold and place it on kitchen paper.

Melt half the butter in a frying pan and when it foams, add the asparagus. Turn the heat down to low and turn the asparagus spears, basting them in the butter. Remove the asparagus from the pan and keep it warm. Melt the remaining butter in the pan, and when it foams, add the mushrooms and sauté them quickly over a high heat. Take the pan off the heat, season the mushrooms lightly and add the chopped chives.

Lay the asparagus spears on a dish and scatter the mushrooms over them. Drizzle with lemon juice and sprinkle over some rocket leaves, then garnish with the shards of crispy cheese. Serve warm.

Cold roast beef with celeriac remoulade

Rôti de bœuf froid et céleri rémoulade

Serves two

400g roast beef

Celeriac remoulade
150ml mayonnaise
2 tsp capers
2 medium cornichons,
    chopped into small dice
400g celeriac
Juice of 1 lemon
20g crème fraiche
Salt and black pepper

Vinaigrette
4 tbsp meat juices
    from the beef
1 tbsp sherry vinegar
1 tsp finely chopped
    flatleaf parsley
½ tbsp finely
    chopped chervil
½ tbsp finely
    chopped tarragon
Salt and black pepper

Serving any beef or lamb left from a roast with a warm dressing made with leftover meat juices is a great way to enjoy it. The cold meat goes perfectly with a celeriac remoulade, spiced up with capers, cornichons and a little crème fraiche. Remoulade is always best made a few hours or even the day before eating, so the flavours have a chance to blend and the celeriac softens.

For the remoulade, put the mayonnaise, capers and cornichons in a bowl and season with salt and pepper. Trim, wash and peel the celeriac, cut it into quarters and grate by hand into a bowl. Immediately sprinkle the grated celeriac with lemon juice and toss to prevent it from browning.

Mix the grated celeriac with the mayonnaise, then taste and check the seasoning. Add the crème fraiche. The remoulade should be served chilled but not too cold.

For the vinaigrette, reheat the juices from the roast beef, add the sherry vinegar and chopped herbs and season to taste.

Carve the beef into thin slices, drizzle the warm vinaigrette on top and serve with the celeriac remoulade on the side.

Roast chicken legs with orange

Cuisses de poulet rôties à l'orange

2 large chicken legs, skin on
1 pinch of cayenne pepper
2 oranges
1 carrot, chopped
    into 2cm cubes
1 celery stick, chopped
2 medium potatoes,
    cut into 2cm cubes
½ leek, sliced
1 onion, chopped
1 garlic clove, chopped
1 tbsp vegetable oil
Juice of 2 oranges
50ml dry white wine
200ml chicken stock
Leaves from 3 thyme sprigs
Salt and black pepper

We all know about duck à l'orange, but this is my chicken version, and I think it's just as good.

Preheat the oven to 200°C/Fan 180°C/Gas 6. Season the chicken legs with salt, pepper and cayenne.

Segment the oranges. Slice the top and bottom off an orange with a sharp knife, then cut away the skin, working from top to bottom and removing all the white pith as well as the skin. Then carefully insert the knife between the membranes to separate the segments and remove them. Do this over a bowl to collect any juice. Repeat with the remaining orange, then set the segments aside.

Put all the vegetables in a roasting tin and sprinkle over the garlic. Drizzle everything with the oil and season, then place the chicken legs on top of the vegetables. Mix the orange juice, plus any extra juice from segmenting the oranges, with the white wine and chicken stock and add this to the roasting tin.

Roast in the oven for about 25–30 minutes, until the chicken legs are cooked through. Remove the chicken and then set it aside to rest for 15 minutes, then put the vegetables back in the oven to finish cooking.

Serve the chicken with the orange segments, vegetables and cooking juices. Garnish with thyme leaves.

Chicken sauté with mushrooms & fresh herbs

Sauté de poulet aux champignons et herbes fraîches

Serves two

300g skinless, boneless
   chicken breasts
2 tbsp goose fat
125g chanterelles or other
   wild mushrooms, cleaned
125g button mushrooms,
   cleaned and halved
1 shallot, finely chopped
2 garlic cloves,
   finely chopped
1 tbsp finely chopped
   flatleaf parsley
Leaves from a fresh
   thyme sprig
200ml chicken stock
2 tbsp butter
2 tbsp crème fraiche
Salt and black pepper

To serve
New potatoes

I think of this sauté recipe as being like a French version of a stir-fry, as the chicken is cut into really small pieces so it cooks quickly. Good with new potatoes or as a topping for baked potatoes. If you can't find chanterelles or other wild mushrooms, use all button mushrooms.

Slice the chicken into small slivers, about 20g each, and season them with salt and pepper. Heat a frying pan and add the goose fat, then fry the seasoned chicken for 2 to 3 minutes until it's all cooked and golden. Remove and set aside.

In the same pan, fry the mushrooms for a few minutes until nicely coloured and season with salt and pepper. Add the shallot and garlic and cook for about 5 minutes over a medium heat.

Put the chicken back in the pan, add the parsley, thyme and stock and quickly bring to the boil. Stir in the 2 tablespoons of butter and the crème fraiche to finish the sauce.

Serve with new potatoes.

Duck leg confit with ceps & seasonal vegetables

Confit de canard aux cèpes

Serves two

2 tbsp olive oil or duck fat
200g ceps (fresh or frozen)
   or seasonal mushrooms,
   cleaned and roughly
   chopped
6–8 cooked, peeled chestnuts
   (vacuum-packed are fine),
   halved
1 shallot, chopped
2 garlic cloves, chopped
1 tbsp chopped parsley
200g Swiss chard
   or rainbow chard
30g butter
2 confit duck legs
   (shop-bought or see p.240)
2 rosemary sprigs
1 tbsp honey
Salt and black pepper

It's fine to use shop-bought duck confit and save yourself some time. Most French people don't confit duck themselves and I'm all in favour of using good labour-saving ingredients, such as confit and vac-packed chestnuts. Someone else has done part of the work for you to help you produce a delicious quick meal.

Heat the olive oil or duck fat in a frying pan and cook the mushrooms until lightly coloured. Turn down the heat and add the chestnuts, shallot, garlic and parsley. Cook for about 5 minutes, until the shallot and garlic are soft.

Chop the Swiss chard, keeping the leaves and stalks separate. Melt the butter in a separate pan along with a drop of water. Add the chard stalks and cook them for one minute, then add the rest of the chopped chard and cook for another minute. Season with salt and pepper.

Meanwhile, place the duck legs in a cold pan, skin-side down, and cook over a low-medium heat for about 10 minutes until golden. Carefully turn the legs over and leave them to cook for another few minutes.

To serve, use the rosemary sprigs to brush the duck legs with honey, then serve with the mushroom and chestnut mixture and the chard.

Sausage, pea & potato casserole

Casserole de pommes de terre, petits pois et saucisse de Toulouse

Serves two

1 large potato, peeled
2 tbsp vegetable oil
4 Toulouse sausages
   (or other good-quality
   sausages)
1 large onion, sliced
1 tbsp plain flour
1 tbsp tomato paste
1 tsp sugar
350ml chicken or
   vegetable stock
200g peas
1 tbsp chopped parsley
Salt and black pepper

It's not just the British who enjoy sausage casseroles – the French love them too – and this dish is easy, quick and filling. I like Toulouse sausages or you might prefer the Italian fennel style or a herby sausage.

Preheat the oven to 200°C/Fan 180°C/Gas 6. Cut the peeled potato into 2cm dice, then season and drizzle with a tablespoon of the oil. Spread the diced potato over a baking tray and place the sausages on top. Bake for about 15 minutes, then remove the sausages and set them aside. Put the potatoes back in the oven for another 10 to 15 minutes until golden and cooked through.

Heat the remaining oil in a pan that's large enough to hold the sausages and cook the onion over a high heat until it's nicely browned. Add the flour, tomato paste and sugar and stir well, then add the stock. Bring to the boil, add the peas and cook for about 5 minutes.

Add the sausages, turn down the heat and simmer for 6 minutes until cooked through. Then add the potatoes and season with salt and pepper. Sprinkle with parsley and serve.

Red rice with merguez sausages

Riz camarguais aux merguez

Serves two

2 tbsp olive oil
1 shallot, chopped
1 garlic clove, chopped
1 rosemary sprig,
    finely chopped
100g red rice, soaked for
    30 minutes, then rinsed
25ml dry white wine
350ml vegetable stock
200g lamb merguez sausages
½ preserved lemon,
    finely chopped
10 cherry tomatoes, halved
Salt and black pepper

Herb pesto
Small handful of
    coriander leaves
Small handful of
    mint leaves
Small handful of
    parsley leaves
5–6 tbsp extra virgin
    olive oil

Red rice from the Camargue region of France takes longer to cook than white rice but it's well worth it for the lovely nutty taste. I use it a lot and enjoy it in this dish with merguez sausages and some herby pesto. Merguez are quick to cook and they have a great spicy flavour. And if you want extra heat, you could add a little chilli.

Heat the oil in a pan and cook the shallot, garlic and rosemary until soft. Add the rice, then the wine and stock and bring to the boil. Turn the heat down to a gentle simmer and cook for about 40 minutes or until the rice is tender and all the liquid has been absorbed.

Meanwhile, make the pesto. Place the herbs in a small food processor along with a little olive oil, then season with salt and pepper to taste. Blitz until smooth.

When the rice has been cooking for about 30 minutes, place a griddle pan over a high heat. When it's hot, add the merguez sausages and cook them for 5–6 minutes, turning regularly until they are charred on all sides.

When the rice is ready, stir in the preserved lemon and the cherry tomatoes, then season to taste. Serve the rice with the merguez sausages and drizzle generously with herby pesto.

Pork steaks with summer vegetables
Steaks de porc aux légumes d'été

2 x 250g rib-eye pork steaks
2 tbsp olive oil
80g patty pan squash,
    cut into wedges
80g yellow courgettes,
    thickly sliced
100g asparagus tips
80g baby courgettes,
    thickly sliced
100g cherry tomatoes
80ml dry white wine
Courgette flowers, stamens
    removed and flowers
    gently torn (optional)
1 tbsp finely chopped sage
1 tbsp finely chopped
    oregano
30g butter
Zest of ½ lemon
Salt and black pepper

*Rib-eye is an unusual cut of pork, but I like it as there is a good
vein of fat running through it that keeps the meat flavourful and juicy.
Ordinary pork chops will also work well, though. In this recipe,
everything is cooked in the same pan so the vegetables pick up
the lovely flavour of the pork. Here we use summer vegetables,
but you can vary the vegetables according to the season.*

Take the steaks out of the fridge about 30 minutes before you
want to start cooking. Season each steak with salt on both sides.

Place a large non-stick frying pan over a high heat. Add a
tablespoon of the olive oil and when the pan is hot, add the
steaks to the pan. Cook the pork for about 5 minutes on each
side or until nicely browned. Remove the steaks from the pan
and set them aside to rest.

Add the remaining olive oil to the pan and add the squash
and yellow courgettes and cook for 2 minutes. Next, add
the asparagus and the baby courgettes and cook for another
1–2 minutes. Add the tomatoes, then pour in the wine to
deglaze the pan. Once the wine begins to bubble, leave it for
about 2 minutes while the alcohol evaporates. Sprinkle over
the courgette flowers, if using, and the herbs, then stir in the
butter and season to taste.

Pour the resting juices from the pork into the frying pan and
add the lemon zest. Serve the pork with the vegetables and the
sauce from the pan.

Barbecued lamb steaks with vegetables & peppercorn sauce

Steak d'agneau au barbecue, légumes et sauce au poivre

Serves two

2 lamb leg or rump steaks,
   at room temperature
2 tbsp vegetable oil
2 green courgettes,
   sliced lengthwise
2 yellow courgettes,
   sliced lengthwise
1 bunch of asparagus,
   trimmed
1 bunch of large
   spring onions
Salt and black pepper

Peppercorn sauce
40g butter
1 shallot, finely chopped
30ml brandy
20ml white wine
100ml beef stock
2 tbsp green peppercorns
100ml double cream
Large pinch of cracked
   black peppercorns

This classic recipe is normally associated with beef but it works just as well with lamb steaks. Just make sure to take your meat out of the fridge at least half an hour before cooking to allow it to come up to room temperature. If you like, you can use a mix of green and pink peppercorns for additional flavour.

Heat the barbecue or a griddle pan until really hot. Brush the steaks with a tablespoon of the oil and season them with salt.

Place the steaks on the hottest part of the barbecue or on the hot griddle pan and cook them for 5–6 minutes on each side for pink meat. The steaks should be seared and even a little charred. Remove them and put them on a plate to rest.

Put all the prepared vegetables on a baking tray, drizzle them with the rest of the oil and season. Mix to coat them with the oil and seasoning, then transfer them to the barbecue or griddle pan. They will cook and char in a few minutes, so keep an eye on them and remove them as soon as they are ready.

For the sauce, heat a frying pan on the barbecue or on the hob and add the butter. When the butter is foaming, add the shallot to the pan and stir until softened. Stir in the brandy and tilt the pan so that the contents flambé. Next add the wine, stock and green peppercorns, pressing down lightly on the peppercorns to release their flavour. Lastly add the cream, cracked black peppercorns and some salt, then take the pan off the heat. Pour any resting juices from the steaks into the sauce. Remove the cooked vegetables from the barbecue or grill pan and set aside.

Serve the steaks with the vegetables and spoon over the delicious peppercorn sauce.

CHAPTER FOUR

MEALS WITH FAMILY & FRIENDS

Repas conviviaux

Quinoa salad with roasted butternut squash, pomegranate & citrus vinaigrette

Salade de quinoa, courge rôtie, grenade et vinaigrette aux agrumes

Serves six

150g red quinoa
150g white quinoa
100g dried apricots,
    soaked for 30 minutes
300g butternut squash,
    peeled and deseeded
Olive oil
50g hazelnuts
50g walnuts
50g cashew nuts
50g sunflower seeds
1–2 tsp honey
2 oranges
100g pomegranate seeds
50g radishes,
    very finely sliced
200g kohlrabi,
    very finely sliced
2 tbsp very finely chopped
    flatleaf parsley
50g watercress
Salt and black pepper

Citrus dressing
90ml lemon juice
1½ tsp caster sugar
200ml cold-pressed
    rapeseed oil

Quinoa is grown in France nowadays and is becoming more and more popular. I enjoy it in this special salad that pleases everyone, vegetarian or not. You can use 750g of ready-cooked quinoa to save time.

First make the dressing. Mix the lemon juice and sugar until the sugar dissolves, then slowly add the rapeseed oil. Season with salt and pepper and set aside.

Cook the red and white quinoa in separate pans according to the packet instructions. Refresh in cold water, then drain and squeeze out any excess water with your hands. Set aside. Drain the apricots, slice them into strips and add them to the quinoa.

Preheat the oven to 200°C/Fan 180°C/Gas 6. Cut the squash into slices about 1cm thick. Toss the slices in olive oil, then place them on a baking tray, season and roast for about 20 minutes until golden brown and soft. Leave to cool.

While the oven is on, line a baking tray with baking paper and spread the nuts and sunflower seeds over it. Drizzle the honey over the nuts and seeds and bake for about 5 minutes until they are caramelised. Remove and leave to cool.

Segment the oranges (see page 86) and set them aside. Add any juice to the quinoa. Mix the quinoa and apricots with the orange segments, pomegranate seeds, radishes, kohlrabi and parsley in a serving dish with the squash and watercress, then garnish with the caramelised seeds and nuts.

Cauliflower & broccoli gratin with Comté cheese

Gratin de chou-fleur et brocoli au vieux Comté

Serves four

1 cauliflower (about 900g)
1 head of broccoli
    (about 400g)
70ml white wine
30ml sherry vinegar
1 banana shallot,
    finely chopped
500ml vegetable stock
1 tbsp cornflour
200ml crème fraiche
100g mature Comté
    cheese, grated
2 free-range egg yolks
Butter, for greasing
40g flaked almonds, toasted
Salt and black pepper

Even more delicious than a regular cauliflower cheese and well worth the effort, this recipe uses the broccoli stalks and cauliflower core as well as the florets, so there's no waste. The different colours of the vegetables make the dish look extra appetising too.

Divide the cauliflower and broccoli into small florets of roughly the same size. Chop the cauliflower core and the broccoli stalks.

Prepare a bowl of iced water. Bring a saucepan of water to the boil and add salt. Add the cauliflower florets, bring the water back to the boil and cook for 2 minutes – the florets should still be crunchy. Remove them with a slotted spoon and add them to the bowl of iced water so they keep their colour, then drain. Cook the broccoli florets in the same way. Lastly, cook the chopped stems and core in the same water for about 3 minutes, transfer them to iced water, then drain.

Put the wine and vinegar in a pan with the shallot and reduce the liquid over a high heat until it is almost a syrup. Add the vegetable stock and continue to cook until reduced by half. Mix the cornflour with a tablespoon of water and add it to the stock. Keep boiling for another 5 minutes until the sauce has thickened, then add the crème fraiche and cook until the sauce has reduced to about 200ml – about 4 medium ladlefuls. Take the sauce off the heat, stir in half the cheese, then the egg yolks. Do not let the sauce boil again.

Butter a gratin dish which has a capacity of about 2.5 litres and add half of the sauce. Add the chopped core and stems, then the florets, making sure you can see both colours, then season. Pour the rest of the sauce over the vegetables and sprinkle with the remaining cheese. Brown the top under a preheated grill or put the dish in a hot oven (240°C/Fan 220°C/Gas 9) until golden. Sprinkle with the almonds and serve.

Courgette gratin
Gratin de courgettes

Serves four to six

60g butter, plus extra
    for greasing
2 tbsp olive oil
2 banana shallots,
    finely chopped
5 or 6 garlic cloves,
    finely chopped
700g courgettes (a variety
    of colours and types if
    possible), grated
40g plain flour
350ml milk
Grating of nutmeg
2 free-range eggs, beaten
200g hard cheese, such as
    Tomme des Pyrénées,
    Comté or hard goat
    cheese, grated
1 green courgette and
    1 yellow courgette,
    thinly sliced
Salt and black pepper

If you can, use different colours and varieties of courgette for this gratin, both for the look of the dish and the flavour. Each type will have a different level of sweetness and bitterness. If you have large courgettes, remove the core and seeds as they can be bitter.

Preheat the oven to 220°C/Fan 200°C/Gas 7 and grease a gratin dish, measuring about 24cm in diameter, with butter.

Heat the oil in a large frying pan, add the shallots and garlic and sauté without allowing them to colour. Add the grated courgettes and sauté until no liquid is left in the pan – this is important as otherwise the gratin will be too watery.

Melt the 60g of butter in a separate pan, stir in the flour to make a roux and cook for a few minutes over a low heat. Add the milk slowly, stirring constantly to avoid lumps. Season the sauce with salt, pepper and a grating of nutmeg and simmer for about 10 minutes.

Take the pan off the heat and add the grated courgettes, eggs and half the cheese, then pour the mixture into the gratin dish. Arrange the sliced courgettes on top, alternating the colours, if possible. Sprinkle with the rest of the cheese and bake for 30 minutes. Serve at once with salad.

106   Meals with family & friends

Roast vegetable tart tatin
Tarte tatin de légumes

Serves four

3 small heads of red chicory
3 small heads of yellow chicory
200g slender carrots,
    halved lengthways
300g kohlrabi, cut into batons
100g cauliflower florets or
    sprouting broccoli, halved
1 large onion, cut into wedges
2 tbsp olive oil
2 tbsp butter
2 tbsp caster sugar
1 red chilli, deseeded
    and sliced
Leaves from 1 thyme sprig
350g puff pastry
Flour, for dusting
Salt and black pepper

Here we have a great French classic made into a vegetarian treat. I've suggested a selection of vegetables, but you can vary them according to the season and spice them up with more chilli if you like a bit of heat. Delicious as a main meal or as an accompaniment, this can be made in individual portions as well as a large tart. It's fine to use shop-bought puff pastry – I do!

Preheat the oven to 220°C/Fan 200°C/Gas 7. Cut the heads of chicory in half (or if they are large, into quarters) and put them in a bowl with the other vegetables. Add the oil and toss, then season with salt and black pepper. Spread the vegetables over a baking tray and roast them in the oven for 8–10 minutes. The vegetables should be partly cooked and have a little colour.

Melt the butter in a large (28cm) ovenproof frying pan, then sprinkle over the sugar. Place the cooked vegetables, sliced chilli and thyme on top, making sure to pack the vegetables tightly.

Roll out the pastry on a floured work surface to 3mm thick. Place the pastry over the vegetables, tucking it in around the edges. Make a few holes in the pastry with the point of a knife, then bake for 20 minutes. Leave to cool a little, then place a plate over the pan and carefully turn the pan over to invert the tart on to the plate. Serve warm.

Roasted sea bass
Loup de mer rôti

Serves four

1 x 1.2kg sea bass,
    gutted and scaled
3 new season's onions
    or large spring onions,
    sliced into 3mm rounds
1 shallot, quartered
4 tbsp olive oil, plus
    extra for finishing
2 bay leaves
8 thyme sprigs
2 tomatoes, sliced
    into thin rounds
4 small courgettes,
    sliced into thin rounds
16 black olives, pitted
1 lemon, sliced into
    thin rounds
500ml dry white wine
3 fresh dill sprigs
Salt and black pepper

I love cooking fish on the bone as it retains all its flavour and texture. Sea bass is a glorious fish and this method of roasting it in the oven is simple but results in an excellent dish.

Preheat the oven to 220°C/Fan 200°C/Gas 7.

Rinse the fish under cold water and dry it with kitchen paper. Spread the onions and shallot over a baking tray and toss them with a tablespoon of the olive oil. Add the bay leaves and half the thyme to the baking tray, then season with salt and pepper.

Season the outside of the fish with 2 generous pinches of salt and a grinding of pepper. Season the cavity in the same way. Lay the fish on top of the onions, shallot and herbs. Put the tomato rounds, courgette slices, olives and lemon into the cavity of the fish and add the remaining thyme. Pour the wine and the rest of the olive oil over the fish.

Bake for 20–30 minutes, depending on the thickness of the fish. It is cooked when the flesh is white and can be easily pulled from the backbone. Carefully place the fish on to a serving platter, drizzle with olive oil and sprinkle with dill.

Serve immediately with all the vegetables and the juices from the baking tray.

Gratin with prawns & salmon

Gratin de saumon et crevettes aux épinards

Serves four

250ml fish stock
450g salmon, skinned
    and cut into 2cm pieces
450g raw prawns,
    peeled and deveined
25ml white wine
175ml whole milk
50ml double cream
50g butter, plus extra
    for greasing
1 leek, trimmed, halved
    lengthways and sliced
25g plain flour
1 tbsp olive oil
1 shallot, finely chopped
1 garlic clove, finely chopped
250g baby spinach
Small handful of flatleaf
    parsley, roughly chopped
40g Comté cheese, grated
Salt and black pepper

The prawns bring a bit of luxury to this beautiful fish gratin and there's a lovely touch of green from the spinach and leek. All the preparation can be done in advance if you like.

Bring the stock to a simmer in a saucepan. Add the salmon and poach for one minute. Then add the prawns and poach for another minute. Remove all the seafood with a slotted spoon and set it aside in a bowl.

Add the wine to the saucepan, bring it to the boil and reduce it for 5 minutes. Add the milk and cream and simmer for a few more minutes.

Meanwhile, melt half the butter in another pan, add the sliced leek and cook for about 5 minutes until soft. Remove the leek and set it aside.

Melt the rest of the butter in the pan. Add the flour, stir it well and then add the milk and stock mixture, a ladleful at a time. Keep stirring until all the liquid is incorporated and the sauce is smooth with no lumps and has slightly thickened. Bring the sauce to the boil, add the cooked leek, then turn down the heat and leave the sauce to simmer for about 15 minutes.

Take a gratin dish which has a capacity of about 2.5 litres and grease it with butter. Preheat the grill to high.

Add the oil to a small pan and cook the shallot and garlic for 2 minutes. Add the spinach and let it wilt, then drain it and squeeze out as much liquid as possible. Season the spinach and add it to the gratin dish, then add the poached fish and prawns. Stir the parsley into the leek sauce, then pour it over the fish.

Sprinkle the grated cheese on top and place the dish under the hot grill for 10 minutes until golden brown and the contents are bubbling. You can prepare the gratin in advance, if you prefer, then bake it in a preheated oven, 200°C/Fan 180°C/Gas 6, for about 15 minutes.

Salmon Wellington
Saumon en croûte

Serves six

200g red rice
2 heads of chicory,
    cut in half or into
    quarters if large
80g unsalted butter
1 tbsp honey
2 tbsp orange juice
1 onion, finely diced
1 radicchio, sliced
400g salmon fillet, cleaned
    pin-boned and skinned
3 buckwheat pancakes
    (see p.240)
320g ready-rolled puff pastry
2 free-range eggs, beaten
Salt and black pepper

To serve
White wine butter sauce
    (see p.236)

A take on the classic beef Wellington, this salmon version is a splendid feast. You could also make a vegetarian version by using salt-baked celeriac or braised leeks instead of salmon.

Soak the rice in cold water for a couple of hours or overnight. Drain the rice, then put it in a pan and cover with water. Bring to the boil and cook for 40 minutes or until tender. Set aside.

Cook the chicory in a pan of salted water until tender, then drain and squeeze out the excess water. Melt a tablespoon of the butter in a pan and sauté the chicory until browned. Add the honey and orange juice to deglaze the pan, then reduce to a syrupy consistency. Set aside.

Melt the rest of the butter in another pan and sweat the onion until translucent. Add the radicchio and cook for a few minutes, then add the cooked rice and stir well. Season and set aside.

Check that there are no pin bones remaining in the salmon. Cut the salmon in half lengthways and season.

Place a sheet of cling film on the work surface, then place the pancakes, side by side and overlapping slightly, on top. Spread the rice mixture over the pancakes, then lay the salmon pieces end to end over the rice. Add the chicory on top of the salmon. Fold the pancakes over the salmon and wrap the parcel tightly in the cling film. Place in the fridge and chill for about an hour.

Preheat the oven to 200°C/Fan 180°C/Gas 6. When the Wellington is well chilled, remove the cling film. Lay the puff pastry sheet on a large baking tray and place the Wellington on one half of the pastry. Fold the pastry over and press the edges together to seal. Brush twice with beaten egg and decorate with the tip of a fork if you wish. Bake for about 35 minutes until golden brown. Serve with the white wine butter sauce.

Plaice poached in cider with mussels, scallops & prawns
Plie à la Normande

Serves four

30g unsalted butter,
    plus extra for greasing
2 shallots, chopped
100ml dry cider, plus 3 tbsp
500g mussels, washed and
    beards and barnacles
    scraped off (discard
    any mussels that don't
    close when tapped)
Juice of 1 lemon
12 small white button
    mushrooms
4 plaice fillets,
    rinsed and dried
4 medium scallops, cleaned
    and trimmed (optional)
500ml fish stock
200ml whipping cream
100g prawns, cooked
    and peeled
2 tbsp chopped parsley,
    to serve
Salt and black pepper

To serve
New potatoes
Spinach

A luxurious way of cooking an underrated fish, this is good served with sautéed spinach and boiled potatoes.

Melt a small knob of the butter in a large pan. Add half the chopped shallots and cook for 2 minutes over a very low heat. Pour the 100ml of cider into the pan, add the mussels and season with pepper. Stir, then cover the pan and cook the mussels over a high heat for 4 minutes, shaking the pan frequently. Take the pan off the heat and drain the mussels in a colander over a bowl to reserve the cooking juices. Remove the mussel flesh from the shells, then pass the cooking juices through a fine sieve into a bowl and set aside.

Heat another knob of butter in a pan with a tablespoon of lemon juice and 4 tablespoons of water. Add the mushrooms and cook them over a high heat for 5 minutes, stirring often. Taste and season with salt and pepper, then set aside.

Preheat the oven to 180°C/Fan 160°C/Gas 4. Take a gratin dish which has a capacity of about 2.5 litres and grease it with butter. Spread the remaining shallots over the base. Season, then fold the plaice fillets in half and put them on top. Add the scallops, if using, and season, then add the fish stock, mussel cooking liquid, the 3 tablespoons of cider and the mushrooms. Cut a piece of baking parchment the size of the dish and butter it, then lay it on top, buttered side down. Bake for 10 minutes.

Remove the dish from the oven. Take out the fish and the scallops, if using, with a slotted spoon. Set them aside on a warm plate and cover tightly with foil. Pour the cooking juices into a pan, bring them to the boil and boil for 10 minutes. Pour in half of the cream and bring to the boil again, then add the prawns and mussels and simmer for a couple of minutes. Whip the rest of the cream until it is quite firm, then fold it into the sauce and add a few drops of lemon juice. Serve the fish and shellfish with the sauce and sprinkle with chopped parsley.

Sea bream baked in a salt crust
Dorade en croûte de sel

Serves four

2 whole sea bream,
  about 750g each,
  cleaned, scaled and
  fins and gills removed
2 thyme sprigs
2 rosemary sprigs
1 tsp chopped
  coriander leaves
1 lemon, sliced
5 egg whites
2kg coarse salt
½ tbsp olive oil
Lemon juice (optional)
Black pepper

Lorette salad
2 Romaine lettuces, shredded
4 celery sticks, chopped
  in batons and tough
  strings removed
2 heads of red chicory,
  each leaf cut lengthways
2 heads of yellow endives,
  each leaf cut lengthways
2 cooked medium beetroot,
  peeled and cut into batons
6 tbsp classic French
  dressing (see p.238)

Encasing fish in a salt crust is a great way of cooking it and it's fun to break the crust open in front of everyone to bring a bit of theatre to the meal. The fish bakes in its own steam and the salt does impart some flavour. Don't use your expensive flaked sea salt, though – cheap salt is fine. Sea bass is also good cooked by this method.

Preheat the oven to 230°C/Fan 210°C/Gas 8. Rinse the fish under cold running water and dry them with kitchen paper. Season the cavity of each fish with 2 grindings of pepper and divide the herbs and slices of lemon between them.

Whisk the egg whites until they form soft peaks, then stir in the coarse salt. Spread a layer of the mixture, about 2cm thick, over the base of a baking tray. Lay the fish on top and cover with the rest of the salt mix. Place in the preheated oven and bake for 45 minutes.

Meanwhile, get the salad ingredients ready in a bowl and prepare the vinaigrette.

Remove the baking tray from the oven. Gently break the salt crust open to reveal the fish, then peel off the skin. Remove the fillets by running a thin, sharp knife around the base of the head of each fish and down the backbone on each side, then carefully lift off the fillets.

Use a pastry brush to sweep off any traces of salt, then season the fillets with pepper, half a tablespoon of olive oil and lemon juice, if using. Dress the salad and serve it with the fish.

Barbecued chicken with summer salad
Poulet au barbecue et salade d'été

6 chicken legs, bone in
1 bay leaf
1 rosemary sprig
2 tbsp Dijon mustard
1 tbsp honey
2 garlic cloves, grated
1 tbsp olive oil
Salt and black pepper

Summer salad
3 red and 3 yellow peppers
2 courgettes, cut into rounds
    about 1cm thick
4 large tomatoes, chopped
1 shallot, finely sliced
1 tbsp red wine vinegar
5 tbsp olive oil
Handful of chopped parsley

Barbecued garlic
Whole head of garlic
Olive oil
1 rosemary sprig
1 thyme sprig
Salt and black pepper

I love the smoky flavour of barbecued chicken, but it's best to precook it to be sure it cooks all the way through on the barbecue. I like to use chicken legs on the bone, as they have more flavour than breasts.

Heat the barbecue. For the barbecued garlic, slice off the top of the garlic bulb with a sharp knife, then place the garlic on a piece of foil large enough to encase it. Drizzle lightly with oil, add the herbs and seasoning, then wrap the garlic tightly in the foil. Place it on the rack of the barbecue away from the flame, close the lid and leave it to roast for 30 minutes until soft.

For the salad, put the peppers on the barbecue or on a griddle pan on the hob. Grill the peppers, turning them until blackened all over. Put them in a bowl, cover them with cling film and leave to steam for a few minutes. Add the courgette slices to the barbecue or griddle and grill until charred and tender. Remove and set aside.

When the peppers are cool enough to handle, scrape off the skins. Slice the peppers and put them in a salad bowl with the courgettes, tomatoes and shallot. Drizzle over the vinegar and oil and toss everything well. Sprinkle with parsley. Squash the flesh out of a few garlic cloves and add them to the salad.

For the chicken, bring a pan of salted water to the boil, add the chicken legs and herbs, then simmer for 10 minutes. Remove the chicken legs and leave them to drain and cool.

Mix the mustard, honey, grated garlic and olive oil and season with salt and pepper. Dry the chicken legs with kitchen paper. Make small incisions in the chicken legs, rub in the mustard mixture, then ideally set aside in a cool place for an hour or so to marinate, although you can cook them straight away. Heat the barbecue or griddle pan and grill the chicken until the meat is cooked through and the skin is charred and crispy. To check, put a knife into the chicken near the bone and make sure there is no blood. Serve with the salad and barbecued garlic.

Roast chicken with lemon & garlic butter
Poulet rôti au beurre à l'ail citronné

Serves four to six

2 onions, finely chopped
1 head of garlic, separated
   into cloves, unpeeled
400g new potatoes,
   parboiled until tender
2–3 tbsp dried breadcrumbs
100g lemon & garlic butter
   (see below), softened
1 free-range chicken
   (about 1.8kg)
Olive oil
100ml white wine
120ml chicken stock
Salt and black pepper

Lemon & garlic butter
75g unsalted butter,
   softened, plus extra
   for cooking the shallot
2 garlic cloves,
   finely chopped
Handful of parsley,
   finely chopped
Juice and zest of 1 lemon
1 large shallot, finely chopped
Salt and freshly ground
   white pepper

To serve
Ratatouille (see p.228)

You can't get a dish that's more French than ratatouille. It's an all-time classic and is great served on its own or with a beautiful roast chicken as here – my idea of heaven! Adding the lemon and garlic butter to the chicken before roasting makes the meat extra moist and juicy. The butter can be made in advance and stored in the fridge or frozen, but do bring it to room temperature before using.

First make the lemon and garlic butter. Mix the 75g of butter with the garlic, parsley, lemon juice and zest in a bowl until combined. Heat a little butter in a pan and gently cook the shallot, then add it to the butter mixture. Season to taste and roll the mixture into a 3cm sausage.

Preheat the oven to 220°C/Fan 200°C/Gas 7. Spread the chopped onions over the base of an ovenproof dish or roasting tin and add the garlic cloves and parboiled potatoes.

Mix the breadcrumbs into the lemon and garlic butter and transfer to a piping bag. Carefully lift the skin of the chicken away from the breast and legs and slide your fingers under the skin. Then take the piping bag and squeeze the butter under the skin over the breast, legs and thighs. Massage with your hands to make sure the butter is evenly spread.

Put any remaining butter into the cavity of the chicken. Truss the legs with butcher's string to keep them in place. Rub the chicken with olive oil, season with salt and pepper and place it on top of the potatoes, garlic and onions. Pour over the white wine and chicken stock and roast for 40 minutes. Reduce the heat to 200°C/Fan 180°C/Gas 6, cover the chicken with foil and cook for another 20 minutes.

Remove the chicken from the oven, tip out any juices from the cavity and set them aside. Cover the chicken with foil and leave to rest for 20 minutes before serving. Carve the chicken and serve with the reheated juices and the ratatouille.

Chicken pithivier
with wild mushrooms

*Pithiviers de volaille
et champignons sauvages*

Serves six

Vegetable oil
1 shallot, finely chopped
400g wild mushrooms
    or button mushrooms,
    cleaned and sliced
2 large boneless, skinless
    chicken breasts
Grating of nutmeg
2 free-range eggs
250ml whipping cream
1 smoked chicken breast
800g puff pastry
Flour, for dusting
Salt and black pepper

To serve
Creamy mushroom sauce
    (see p.232)

A pithivier is a classic French puff pastry-topped pie that can be sweet or savoury. This version is filled with chicken breasts and mushrooms, and if you're feeling extravagant you could add a truffle. Using a smoked chicken breast adds extra flavour, but you might need to order one from your butcher. You can prepare the filling the day before.

Heat a little oil in a pan and fry the shallot and mushrooms over a medium heat until softened. Remove and drain off any liquid, then set them aside to cool.

Trim the chicken breasts and cut them into cubes, making sure you remove any fat. Put the chicken in a food processor and blitz to make a fine purée. Season generously with salt and pepper and a grating of nutmeg, then add the white of one of the eggs and the cream. Blitz again until smooth.

Dice the smoked chicken meat and fold it into the chicken purée. Beat the egg yolk with the remaining egg and set aside.

Preheat the oven to 200°C/Fan 180°C/Gas 6. Roll out the puff pastry on a floured surface and cut it into 2 rounds about 30cm in diameter. Place one of the rounds on a large baking tray (about 30 x 40cm in size). Add half the chicken mixture, leaving a 4cm border all around it, then add the mushroom mixture. Top with the remaining chicken.

Brush the border with beaten egg and place the other circle of pastry on top. Press down well to seal. Trim the edges and brush the pie with egg. Using the tip of a sharp knife, score curved lines in the pastry, from the centre to the edges, working all round the pie. Be careful not to cut right through the pastry. Make a small hole in the top to release steam.

Bake in the oven for 45 minutes. Serve warm or cold with the creamy mushroom sauce.

Poussins braised in red wine

Coquelets braisés au vin rouge

Serves six

3 poussins (about 400g each)
1 litre full-bodied red wine
200g smoked bacon
   in one piece
2 tbsp olive oil,
   plus extra for frying
1 onion, roughly chopped
1 carrot, roughly chopped
1 celery stick,
   roughly chopped
1 garlic clove
1 bouquet garni
2 tbsp plain flour
300ml port
1 litre chicken stock
18 small button mushrooms,
   stalks trimmed
18 button onions
50g butter
1 tbsp chopped
   flatleaf parsley
Salt and black pepper

A wonderful version of the classic coq au vin, this is made with little poussins. Note that the chicken has to be marinated for two to three days before cooking. Lovely served with mashed potatoes (page 229).

Ask your butcher to cut each poussin in half lengthways, then cut off the backbone and wing tips to make 6 leg and breast portions. Put them in a stainless steel or glass container, pour over enough wine to cover, then refrigerate for 2–3 days.

Put the bacon in a pan of cold water, bring to the boil and boil for 5 minutes. Remove and refresh under cold water, then drain. Cut it into lardons 2cm long x 5mm thick and set aside.

Drain the chicken pieces and pat them dry with kitchen paper. Pour the marinade wine into a pan, bring it to the boil and skim well. Heat 2 tablespoons of oil in a large, flameproof casserole dish and sear the chicken all over. Remove and set aside. Add the onion, carrot, celery, garlic and bouquet garni to the dish and cook until well caramelised. Add the flour and stir for 3 minutes. Pour in the marinade wine, plus any wine left in the bottle, then add the port and bring to the boil. Cook, stirring regularly, until the liquid is reduced by half.

Put the chicken back in the dish, add the stock and bring to a simmer. Cover with a piece of greaseproof paper and put the dish in the oven at 140°C/Fan 120°C/Gas 1 for one hour. When the chicken is nearly ready, fry the bacon lardons in a little oil until golden but still moist and set them aside to keep warm. Fry the mushrooms in a little oil until lightly coloured, season and set aside. Fry the button onions gently in oil and a little of the butter until golden, then drain and set aside.

Remove the chicken from the dish and cover with foil to keep warm. Add the onions to the dish and boil for 5 minutes, then add the mushrooms and simmer for another 5 minutes. Whisk in the rest of the butter and check seasoning. Put the chicken back in the dish and add the lardons and parsley on top.

Chicken with honey & rosemary baked in a salt crust

Poulet au miel et romarin en croûte de sel

Serves four to six

2 tbsp clear honey
Good pinch of paprika
1 good-quality chicken,
    about 1.8kg in weight
Salt and black pepper

Stuffing
4 chicken livers
100g mixed dried
    mushrooms, soaked in a
    bowl of water overnight
2 tbsp butter
6 pure meat pork sausages,
    skins removed
2 tbsp fresh breadcrumbs
1 bunch of chives, chopped
1 free-range egg, beaten

Salt crust
1kg plain flour
2 egg whites
3 tbsp chopped rosemary
250g fine table salt
400g coarse sea salt
1 free-range egg, beaten

A showstopper of a dish, this is a great alternative to the traditional roast. You need to start preparations the day before you want to cook.

Season the honey with paprika and black pepper, then brush it all over the chicken. This is best done on the day before cooking and repeated 2 or 3 times with the same mixture. Keep the chicken in the fridge. To make the salt crust, mix the flour, egg whites and rosemary with 450ml of water to form a paste. Add both kinds of salt and knead for 5 minutes, then wrap the salt dough in cling film and refrigerate.

To make the stuffing, cut the livers into large dice. Drain, rinse and chop the mushrooms. Heat the butter in a pan until it foams, then add the mushrooms and cook for 5–6 minutes. Add the livers and cook, stirring, for 2–3 minutes. Remove the pan from the heat, tip the livers and mushrooms into bowl and leave them to cool. Once cool, mix in the sausage meat, then the breadcrumbs, chives and egg. Take the chicken out of the fridge 30 minutes before you want to cook it and fill the cavity with the stuffing. Preheat the oven to 220°C/200°C/Gas 7.

Roll out the salt dough. Cut it into 2 pieces, one large enough to place the chicken on with a border all the way round. The other piece should be slightly bigger, so it can be draped over the chicken and seal it completely. Place the chicken on the smaller piece of dough, then cover with the remaining piece. Press around the edges to seal and brush with beaten egg.

Bake for one hour, then remove and leave to rest for 40 minutes before breaking open the crust. To do this, cut around the side of the crust with a sharp serrated knife and lift off the top so you can remove the chicken. Discard the salt crust. Carve the chicken and serve with some roast potatoes or a light salad.

Duck casserole with thyme
Cassoulet au canard

Serves six

4 tbsp olive oil
2 onions, finely chopped
6 garlic cloves,
   3 finely chopped
500g Tarbais beans,
   soaked overnight
   (or use cannellini
   or haricot beans)
4 bay leaves
4 fresh thyme sprigs,
   plus extra to garnish
4 fresh rosemary sprigs
6 confit duck legs
   (shop-bought
   or see p.240)
6 Toulouse sausages
   (or good-quality
   pork sausages)
1 carrot, finely chopped
1 celery stick, finely chopped
200g smoked bacon lardons
1 tbsp tomato purée
200ml dry white wine
500ml chicken stock
Large handful of flatleaf
   parsley, chopped
50g fresh breadcrumbs
Salt and black pepper

A proper hearty meal, this is warming, nourishing and full of flavour.

Heat the oil in a large pan. Add half the onions and the finely chopped garlic and cook gently for 2 minutes. Drain the beans and add them to the pan with half the bay leaves, thyme and rosemary. Add water to cover generously and bring to the boil. Partially cover the pan, reduce the heat and simmer for 1½ hours until the beans are just tender. Drain the beans, keeping the onions and garlic, and reserve 500ml of the cooking liquid.

Meanwhile, heat a deep flameproof casserole dish over a high heat. Add the duck legs and fry them, skin-side down, for about 5 minutes until crisp. Set them aside and pour off most of the fat from the pan. Add the sausages to the casserole dish and fry them in the duck fat for 5 minutes until browned all over. Remove and set aside with the duck legs.

Add the rest of the onions to the dish with the carrot, celery and lardons and cook, stirring occasionally, for 10 minutes until the vegetables are soft and the lardons are golden. Peel 2 of the remaining garlic cloves and add them to the casserole dish with the tomato purée, then cook for a minute.

Heat the oven to 140°C/Fan 120°C/Gas 1. Pour the wine into the dish, bring to a simmer, then continue cooking until the wine has reduced by about half. Stir in the stock, 500ml of the bean cooking liquid, the remaining bay leaves and thyme and the cooked beans, then season well. Put the duck legs, skin-side up, and the sausages back in the casserole dish, then cover the dish with a lid and bake in the oven for 30 minutes.

Crush the remaining garlic clove and mix it with the chopped parsley and breadcrumbs, then season with salt and pepper. Remove the lid from the casserole dish and sprinkle the parsley mixture over the top. Put the dish back in the oven, uncovered, and bake for another 20–25 minutes more until the top is golden. Serve scattered with extra thyme.

Roast guinea fowl breasts
Suprêmes de pintade rôtis

Serves four

1 tbsp olive oil
4 boneless guinea fowl breasts
    (supremes), skin on
1 banana shallot,
    finely chopped
3 garlic cloves,
    finely chopped
40g butter
100g mixed olives, pitted
8 sundried tomatoes
    (from a jar), cut into quarters
120ml rosé wine
500ml chicken stock
20g cold butter, diced
Handful of fresh basil leaves,
    roughly chopped
Salt and black pepper

Roasted new potatoes
500g new potatoes
1 thyme sprig
1 tbsp olive oil
Salt and black pepper

Guinea fowl is not gamey, but it does have a more pronounced flavour than chicken and is perfect for this recipe. You could substitute chicken or even pheasant, though, if you can't get guinea fowl. I like to use rosé wine here, as it has something of the richness of red wine with the acidity and freshness of white.

First, prepare the potatoes. Preheat the oven to 200°C/Fan 180°C/Gas 6. Put the potatoes in a bowl, add the thyme and olive oil and season with salt and pepper, then toss to coat in the oil. Tip them into a roasting tin and roast for about 30 minutes until golden brown and soft in the middle – large new potatoes might need to cook for longer.

For the guinea fowl, add the olive oil to a non-stick sauté pan and place over a medium heat. Season the breasts on both sides, then put them in the pan, skin-side down. Cook them gently so that the fat from the skin renders slowly. After about 5 or 6 minutes, or once the guinea fowl breasts have browned well on the skin side, turn them over and cook on the flesh side for another 5 or 6 minutes. Remove them from the pan and leave to rest on a plate.

Add the shallot and garlic to the pan along with the 40g of butter. Stir well until they begin to caramelise, then stir in the olives and sundried tomatoes. Add the wine and leave it to simmer for a few minutes before adding the stock. Bring it back up to a simmer and allow it to reduce for a few minutes, then stir in the 20g of cold diced butter. Remove the sauce from the heat and stir in some fresh basil.

Serve the guinea fowl with the roasted new potatoes and spoon the sauce over the top.

Braised duck legs
Cuisses de canard braisées

Serves four

4 large duck legs
1 pinch of paprika
2 tbsp vegetable oil
100g ventrèche or
    unsmoked streaky
    bacon, cut into lardons
2 onions, chopped
2 carrots, chopped
    into 2cm cubes
½ celeriac, chopped
    into 2cm cubes
2 shallots, chopped
2 garlic cloves, chopped
1 leek, thinly sliced
1 thyme sprig
1 rosemary sprig
2 tbsp tomato purée
200ml red wine
40ml Madeira
600ml chicken stock
600ml beef stock
Salt and black pepper

Any braised meat is always better cooked in advance and chilled, then reheated and served the following day. This dish does take a while to cook but it's easy to prepare and well worth the effort.

Trim the excess fat from the duck legs and season them with salt, pepper and paprika. Preheat the oven to 180°C/ Fan 160°C/Gas 4.

Heat the vegetable oil in a flameproof casserole dish, add the seasoned duck legs and fry them until they are nice and golden on all sides. Remove and set aside.

Add the bacon lardons and the vegetables, except the leek, to the casserole dish and fry over a medium heat until golden and caramelised. Add the leek, thyme, rosemary and tomato purée, then cook over a low heat until the leek is soft. Don't allow the leek to brown or it will turn bitter.

Put the duck legs back in the pan, add the red wine and Madeira to deglaze and cook over a medium heat until the liquid has reduced and is syrupy. Add the chicken stock and beef stock, bring them to the boil and season with salt and pepper. Cover with a piece of baking parchment and a lid, then put the dish in the oven and braise until the meat is tender and just about falling off the bone. This will take about 2 hours, depending on the size of the duck legs.

When the duck legs are ready, carefully remove them from the pan. Push the sauce through a sieve, pressing the vegetables well, and season. Serve the duck legs with plenty of sauce and perhaps some crushed potatoes (see page 231) and roast carrots (see page 229).

Pheasant pie with mushrooms
Parmentier de faisan aux champignons

Serves six

4 pheasants
40g Maldon sea salt
1 tsp white peppercorns
2 thyme sprigs
2 bay leaves, torn
1kg duck fat
4 shallots, finely chopped
Leaves from a few
    thyme sprigs
300g wild mushrooms
    or seasonal mushrooms
175ml red wine
400ml chicken stock
Handful of flatleaf
    parsley, chopped
Salt and black pepper

Topping
1kg floury potatoes,
    cut into 5cm chunks
100–125ml warm milk
150–200g Comté cheese,
    grated

Confit pheasant is unusual but it works a treat and this fancy version of shepherd's pie is something I always cook in game season. You do need to start preparing the pheasants the day before making the pie.

Joint the pheasants into breasts and legs (or ask your butcher to do this for you). Put the pieces in a bowl and add the sea salt, peppercorns and herbs. Cover with cling film and leave to marinate overnight in the fridge. The next day, dry the pheasant joints with kitchen paper.

Preheat the oven to 140°C/Fan 120°C/Gas 1. Melt the duck fat in an ovenproof pan on the hob. Add the pheasant joints and gently bring the fat to a simmer. Place the pan in the oven and cook for 2–3 hours until tender – the fat must not bubble. Check after about 2 hours and if the meat comes off the bone easily, the pheasant joints are ready.

Leave them until cool enough to handle, then strip off all the meat and shred it with your fingers. Discard the skin and bones. Pour the fat into clean jam jars. You will need some for finishing this dish, but save the rest for roasting potatoes another day.

Heat 2 tablespoons of the fat in a saucepan. Add the shallots, thyme and mushrooms, then season with pepper. Cook gently until the shallots are soft, then add the wine and stock. Bring to the boil, then simmer until the liquid has reduced by half and has a sauce-like consistency. Add the pheasant meat and chopped parsley, then check the seasoning.

For the topping, boil the potatoes in salted water for 20–25 minutes until tender. Drain well, then mash until smooth. Add the warm milk and 200g of the confit fat. Preheat the oven to 230°C/Fan 210°C/Gas 8. Grease a baking dish, about 30 x 20cm in size, with duck fat. Pile in the meat mixture and cover with the mashed potatoes. Sprinkle the cheese on top and bake for about 25 minutes or until heated through and browned on top. Serve with a green salad or vegetables.

Quiche Lorraine
Quiche Lorraine

Serves four to six

Pastry
125g cold butter, diced,
 plus extra for greasing
250g plain flour, plus
 extra for dusting
1 tsp salt
1 medium free-range egg

Filling
250g salt pork belly or
 streaky bacon (smoked
 or unsmoked or a mixture),
 cut into small lardons
1 tbsp oil
3 medium free-range eggs
6 medium free-range
 egg yolks
Grating of nutmeg
500ml double cream
2 tbsp kirsch
200g Gruyère or Comté
 cheese, coarsely grated
Salt and black pepper

A French classic, this is rich in cheese, eggs and cream, but I say, you can't skimp on a quiche. The addition of kirsch is an Alsace tradition.

Grease a deep, fluted tart tin, about 25cm in diameter, with butter and dust it with flour. To make the pastry, put the butter into a mixing bowl and add the flour and salt. Using your fingertips, mix the butter into the flour, but do not overwork it. When the mixture has a sandy texture, add the egg to it and bring the dough together.

Place the dough on a floured work surface and knead it a few times to make it completely smooth. Roll it out into a round, about 3mm thick, and use it to line the tart tin, allowing it to overhang the edges. Prick the base with a fork, then line with baking parchment and add baking beans. Leave to rest in the fridge for at least 20 minutes. Preheat the oven to 200°C/Fan 180°C/Gas 6. Bake the pastry case for about 20 minutes, then remove the beans and paper and bake for another 10 minutes.

Bring a pan of water to the boil and add the lardons, then bring the water back to the boil and drain them. Put the lardons in a non-stick frying pan with the tablespoon of oil and brown them over a medium heat for a few minutes until caramelised but not dry. Remove the lardons and drain off some fat, then set aside.

Lightly whisk the whole eggs and extra yolks in a jug and season with salt, pepper and nutmeg. Add the cream and the kirsch, then most of the grated cheese. Arrange the lardons in the baked pastry case. Pour in about three-quarters of the filling, then place the dish in the oven and fill it right to the top with the rest of the filling mixture. Sprinkle the remaining cheese on top. Lower the oven setting to 190°C/Fan 170°C/Gas 5 and bake for 20–30 minutes until the quiche is golden brown and firm in the middle – give it a little longer if necessary. Remove from the oven and carefully trim the edges of the pastry. Gently remove the quiche and serve warm or tepid, but not piping hot, as it's easier to slice when it has cooled a little.

Spiced lamb shoulder with couscous
Épaule d'agneau aux épices et couscous

4 garlic cloves, chopped
2 tsp ground cinnamon
2 tsp ground cumin
1 tbsp dried oregano
1 lemon, quartered,
    pips removed
1 tsp salt
2 tsp ground black pepper
1 lamb shoulder
2 red onions, cut into wedges
1 litre pomegranate juice
200ml lamb or chicken stock
150g couscous
400g tin of chickpeas,
    drained and rinsed
100g tub of pomegranate
    seeds, or seeds from
    1 fresh pomegranate
Small handful of mint
    leaves, chopped
100ml olive oil
2 tbsp clear honey
50ml lemon juice

Garnish
Extra pomegranate seeds
    and mint leaves

The inspiration for this dish comes from North African cooking and I use spices normally associated with tagines. The lamb does have to be marinated for up to two days and needs long, slow cooking, but you are rewarded with flavourful meat that's falling off the bone. Perfect with the couscous and chickpeas.

Put the garlic, cinnamon, cumin, oregano and lemon quarters in a blender with the salt and black pepper, then blend until smooth. Put the lamb shoulder in a large roasting tin and tip the marinade over the top. Massage the marinade all over the lamb and leave it in the fridge for 24 hours or up to 2 days.

Remove the lamb from the fridge about an hour before cooking. Preheat the oven to 160°C/Fan 140°C/Gas 3. Scatter the onion wedges around the lamb, tucking some underneath, then pour over the pomegranate juice and the stock. Cover the lamb with a piece of baking paper, then some foil and cook for 4 hours until the meat is nice and tender. Remove the lamb from the oven and set it aside to rest. Reserve the cooking juices.

Put the couscous and chickpeas in a mixing bowl and add 300ml of the lamb cooking juices. Leave to stand until the couscous has absorbed all the liquid, then break it up with a fork. Add the pomegranate seeds and mint leaves and stir in the olive oil.

Drizzle the honey and lemon juice over the lamb, garnish with pomegranate seeds and mint leaves, and serve with the couscous and chickpeas.

Lamb casserole with spring vegetables
Navarin d'agneau aux légumes de printemps

Serves six

1.2kg lamb neck fillet,
    trimmed and cut
    into 60g pieces
50g olive oil
2 large carrots,
    roughly chopped
2 small onions,
    roughly chopped
40g flour
300ml dry white wine
4 large ripe tomatoes,
    peeled, deseeded
    and chopped
3 garlic cloves, crushed
1.5 litres lamb or
    chicken stock
1 bouquet garni
Salt and black pepper

Garnish
18 baby carrots, peeled
18 baby turnips, peeled
18 baby onions, peeled
200g peas
Chopped flatleaf parsley

To serve
Mashed potato with cream
    (see p.229)

What could be more delicious than lamb with the new season's spring vegetables? This classic is a family favourite but also a dish that was on the menu at Le Gavroche for many years.

Season the lamb with salt and pepper. Heat the oil in a large flameproof casserole dish, add a batch of lamb and sauté until golden brown on all sides – don't add too much meat at a time or it will steam and not brown. Remove the meat from the pan and set aside, then repeat until all the lamb is browned. Preheat the oven to 180°C/Fan 160°C/Gas 4.

Remove the excess fat from the pan, then add the carrots and onions and sweat until soft. Stir in the flour and cook gently for 2 minutes, stirring with a spatula. Pour in the white wine and bring to a simmer, then add the tomatoes and garlic and cook for a few more minutes. Add the stock and bouquet garni and return the lamb to the pan. Bring to a simmer, skim off any fat from the surface, then cover with a lid and cook in the oven for 45 minutes to an hour.

Remove the casserole dish from the oven and leave to cool for 15 minutes. Using a slotted spoon, lift the meat out of the sauce and set it aside in a bowl. Strain the sauce through a fine sieve into a saucepan. Skim off the excess fat, then place the pan over the heat and reduce the sauce by half. Check the seasoning, then put the meat back in the sauce and reheat gently.

Cook all the baby vegetables and the peas separately in salted boiling water until tender. Add the vegetables to the lamb and simmer for another 5 minutes, then sprinkle with parsley and serve. Nice with mashed potatoes.

Roast pork & crispy ears
Rôti de porc et ses oreilles croustillantes

Serves six

2.5kg boned and rolled
    pork shoulder
Vegetable oil
2 onions, sliced
2 garlic cloves, crushed
2 thyme sprigs
2 sage sprigs
1 bay leaf
500ml chicken stock
2 shallots, finely chopped
3 apples, peeled and diced
200ml dry white wine
200ml cider
100ml calvados
1 tbsp wholegrain mustard
2 tbsp butter
Salt and black pepper

Trotters and ears
3 pigs' hind trotters
3 pigs' ears (optional)
Black peppercorns
1 bay leaf
Vegetable oil, for frying
Flour, for dusting
Pinch of celery salt
Pinch of garlic powder
Pinch of smoked paprika
Pinch of piment d'espelette
    or chilli flakes

I cook this regularly for the family and in France I use a cut of pork from the leg called a 'rouelle'. In the UK, though, I make it with boned and rolled pork shoulder which works fine. I do love the crispy, deep-fried ears but they are, of course, optional.

Burn off any hairs from the trotters and ears, if using, with a blowtorch. Place the trotters and ears in a pan of cold water and add a few peppercorns and a bay leaf and season with salt. Bring to a gentle simmer, then partly cover with a lid and cook for 3 hours or until tender. Drain and set the liquid aside. Shred the meat from the trotters and cut the ears into strips.

Preheat the oven to 200°C/Fan 180°C/Gas 6. Put the pork in a large roasting tin with a couple of tablespoons of oil and sear it on both sides. Season and add the onions, garlic, thyme, sage and bay leaf. Pour in the stock and 500ml of water, then roast the pork for about 2 hours, depending on the thickness of the joint. Remove the pork and leave it to rest for at least 20 minutes in a warm place.

Drain the juices from the tin into a bowl, press them through a sieve and set aside. Put the roasting tin back on the heat, add a little oil and the shallots and diced apples. When they are softened, add the wine, cider and calvados to deglaze the pan, then boil until the liquid has reduced by half. Add 300ml of the trotter cooking liquid, the reserved pan juices, the trotter meat, wholegrain mustard and butter. Cook until the sauce has a nice consistency – not too thick, but not too runny. Season to taste.

If cooking the ears, half fill a large pan or a deep-fat fryer with vegetable oil. Dust the ears in flour and deep-fry until crisp and golden. Season with sea salt, celery salt, garlic powder, paprika and piment d'espelette or chilli flakes. Carve the pork at the table and serve with the deep-fried pigs' ears and the sauce, with perhaps pommes anna (page 230) or potatoes dauphinoise (see page 204).

Daube of pork or veal cheeks
Daube de porc ou de veau

Serves six

50g plain flour
12 veal or pork cheeks
100ml vegetable oil
200g carrots, diced
200g celery sticks, diced
200g onions, diced
1 bottle of dry white wine
2 litres veal stock
1 litre tomato passata
1 bouquet garni
200g button onions, peeled
150g smoked bacon,
    cut into lardons
200g ceps or button
    mushrooms
1 tbsp butter
2 tbsp finely chopped
    flatleaf parsley
Salt and black pepper

To serve
Mashed potato with cream
    (see p.229)

A daube is actually a cooking pot but refers to a dish that is cooked for hours in the oven. It's as classic as beef bourguignon. Cheeks are an underused cut but perfect here and you can use pork or veal. This is at its best when made the day before and reheated – the flavour develops as the meat rests in the sauce. Lovely with mash to soak up the juices.

Season the flour with salt and pepper. Trim any excess fat off the cheeks and dust them in seasoned flour. Heat 50ml of the oil in a flameproof casserole dish and fry the cheeks until golden, then remove them and set aside. Preheat the oven to 200°C/Fan 180°C/Gas 6.

Add the diced carrots, celery and onions to the same pan and sauté until brown. Add the wine to deglaze the pan, then cook until it is reduced by half. Add the stock, passata and bouquet garni, then bring to the boil and put the cheeks back in the pan.

Skim any scum off the surface, cover the dish with a lid and braise in the oven for about 1–1½ hours until the meat is beautifully soft and tender.

Meanwhile, heat the rest of the oil in a frying pan. Add the button onions, bacon lardons and mushrooms and cook until caramelised. Add the butter to the pan.

Serve the veal or pork cheeks with the sauce and garnish with the onions, lardons and mushrooms and the chopped parsley.

Beef with bone marrow & vegetables
Pot-au-feu

Serves four

1kg beef shin in one piece
20g coarse salt
200g carrots,
    roughly chopped
200g turnips,
    roughly chopped
100g parsnips,
    roughly chopped
100g celery,
    roughly chopped
2 garlic cloves, cut in half
2 onions, unpeeled,
    cut in half
4 Toulouse sausages
4 pieces of bone marrow,
    in the bones and cut
    into rounds – ask your
    butcher to cut them
    for you (optional)
Handful of chopped parsley
Salt and black pepper

The literal translation of 'pot-au-feu' is pot on the fire and this is a very traditional peasant dish. You would have a big pot of broth simmering away and add whatever cheap cut of meat and vegetables you had to hand. It's a great winter dish and a favourite in my family. Any meat that's left over is good served with a shallot vinaigrette for lunch and the wonderful broth is almost a meal in itself.

Put the meat into a large heavy-based pan, add 4.5 litres of water and the salt, then slowly bring to the boil. Simmer for about 30 minutes, skimming away any scum or fat that comes to the surface.

Add the carrots, turnips, parsnips, celery and garlic, then continue to simmer, uncovered, for 1 hour and 10 minutes. Brown the onion halves in a frying pan without any oil, until burned, then add them to the pot.

Add the sausages and bone marrow, if using, and cook for another 20 minutes. Remove all the meat, then skim off any fat on the surface of the broth. Season to taste.

Ladle the broth and vegetables into big warm bowls. Peel the browned onions and serve one half in each bowl. Cut up the meat and divide it and the sausages and bone marrow, if using, between the bowls. Sprinkle with chopped parsley.

Serve with a strong, Dijon-style mustard and cornichons.

Roast loin of venison with grand veneur sauce & chestnut purée

Longe de chevreuil rôtie, sauce grand veneur et purée de marrons

Serves six

1 x 2kg saddle of venison
(ask your butcher to
remove the loins from
the saddle and chop
the bones)
500ml red wine
3 tbsp redcurrant jelly
1 litre veal stock
2 tbsp olive oil
2 tsp cracked peppercorns
3 tbsp double cream

Marinade
500ml red wine
50ml red wine vinegar
20ml brandy
1 carrot, diced
1 onion, chopped
1 celery stick, chopped
2 garlic cloves, chopped
1 thyme sprig
2 bay leaves
1 clove
5 juniper berries

Chestnut purée
300g cooked and
peeled chestnuts
(vacuum-packed are fine)
240ml whipping cream
240ml white chicken stock
(see p.244)

To serve
Potatoes dauphinoise
(see p.204)

Venison loin is a prime cut and here I marinate it, then I use the marinade to make this classic, very special sauce. The chestnut purée adds the perfect touch of sweetness. You need to start this dish the day before you want to serve it.

Trim any fat and sinew off the loins. Mix all the marinade ingredients together in a large bowl. Add the loins and bones, cover and refrigerate them for 2 hours. Remove the loins from the marinade and set them aside, then leave the bones and any trimmings to marinate overnight.

Preheat the oven to 220°C/Fan 200°C/Gas 7. Drain the bones, trimmings and vegetables from the marinade, put them in a roasting tin and roast for about 30 minutes until golden. Reserve the marinade.

Remove the tin from the oven, place it on the hob and add the marinade liquid to deglaze the pan. Reduce the 500ml of red wine by half in a large saucepan, then add the contents of the roasting tin, plus the redcurrant jelly and veal stock. Simmer for a couple of hours, skimming the surface regularly. Pass everything through a sieve, then pour the liquid back into the pan and reduce until it is sauce consistency. Keeping the pan over the heat, season the sauce with salt to taste and add the cracked peppercorns and double cream.

For the chestnut purée, put everything in a pan and simmer for 5 minutes. Tip it all into a blender and blitz until smooth.

Season the venison loins with salt and pepper. Heat a frying pan with oil, add the loins and cook for 5 minutes on each side. Remove and leave them to rest for about 10 minutes.

Carve the venison and serve it with the sauce, chestnut purée and potatoes dauphinoise.

Venison Wellington with tenderstem broccoli

Chevreuil en croûte et jeunes pousses de brocoli

Serves four

1 tbsp vegetable oil
600g venison loin, cleaned
   and sinew removed
1kg spinach
Flour, for dusting
500g ready-rolled puff pastry
1 free-range egg, beaten
Salt and black pepper

Mushroom duxelles
1 tbsp butter
400g button mushrooms
50g shallots,
   finely chopped
2 garlic cloves,
   finely chopped
100ml Madeira
25ml double cream

Pancakes
110g plain flour
2 free-range eggs
105ml whole milk
1 tbsp vegetable oil

To serve
1 tbsp olive oil
400g tenderstem broccoli
Red wine sauce
   (see p.236 – optional)

Venison is a great alternative to beef and is a lean and healthy meat. I love anything 'en croûte' and although there is quite a bit of preparation for this dish, most of it can done beforehand. It is a delicious feast and is well worth your time.

First, sear the venison loin. Heat the oil in a large frying pan, season the meat with salt and pepper and add it to the pan. Brown it on all sides, turning it every 1–2 minutes until it is evenly coloured and rare in the centre. Remove the meat from the pan, leave it to cool, then put it in the fridge.

Bring a pan of water to the boil and add the spinach. Drain it, then cool in iced water, then drain again. Put the spinach in a tea towel and squeeze until it is as dry as possible. Set aside.

For the duxelles, melt the butter in the same pan that you browned the venison in, add the chopped mushrooms and sauté them until golden brown. Remove them from the pan and set aside, then add the shallots and chopped garlic. Cook until soft, then put the mushrooms back in the pan and cook quickly until the liquid evaporates. Add the Madeira and boil until it has reduced by half. Add the cream and cook until the mixture has thickened and begun to darken. Season with salt and pepper and set aside.

For the pancakes, whisk together the flour, eggs and milk to make a smooth batter. Heat a frying pan and add a drop of oil. Once the oil is hot, pour in a small amount of batter to cover the base in a very thin layer and cook until the pancake is golden on the underside. Flip the pancake over and cook the other side. Repeat to make 2 more, keeping the cooked pancakes to one side.

Lay a sheet of cling film, measuring about 30 x 20cm, on a board and lay the 3 pancakes on it, overlapping them so that they cover the cling film. Lay the spinach leaves on top of the pancakes in a single layer.

Spread the mushroom duxelles over the spinach in an even layer and place the venison on top. Roll the pancakes with the spinach and mushroom mix around the venison, using the cling film to wrap it tightly. Chill in the fridge, preferably overnight.

Preheat the oven, to 180°C/Fan 160°C/Gas 4. On a floured work surface, roll the puff pastry out into a thin sheet, about 2–3mm thick. Remove the Wellington from the cling film, lay it on top of the pastry and brush the borders of the pastry with beaten egg. Roll the Wellington in the pastry, so the join is on the underside and seal it with more beaten egg.

Cook the Wellington in the oven for 20–25 minutes, until the pastry is golden brown. Check that it is cooked by inserting a thin metal skewer in the centre of the venison – it should be slightly warm, which means the internal temperature is about 48–50°C. Remove the Wellington from the oven and leave it to rest for at least 10 minutes in a warm place.

While the venison is resting, cook the broccoli. Heat a frying pan and add the oil, then pan fry the broccoli until golden brown and tender. Season with salt and pepper.

Slice the Wellington and serve it with the broccoli and perhaps a red wine sauce.

Game pâté with black pudding
Pâté de gibier et boudin noir

Serves six to eight

70g chicken livers
1 pheasant breast
40g smoked bacon
200g pork loin
200g venison loin
200g pork back fat
Olive oil
200g mixed wild mushrooms,
    cleaned and sliced
200g shallots, finely sliced
2 thyme sprigs
½ tsp finely chopped
    rosemary
Generous pinch
    of ground cloves
Pinch of ground mace
Pinch of ground juniper
Generous grinding of
    black pepper
20ml Madeira
40ml port
20g green peppercorns
100g pistachio nuts
2 free-range eggs, beaten
100g black pudding,
    sliced into cubes
200g caul fat 'crépinette'
Salt and black pepper

To serve
Chicory salad (see p.228)
    or green salad

A home-made terrine is full of flavour and is a real treat. This is great as part of a special meal or just to have in the fridge for lunch.

Clean the chicken livers, removing any bloody parts. Put them through the medium disc of a mincer with the pheasant breast. Then mince the smoked bacon, pork loin, 100g of the venison loin and the back fat – you could ask your butcher to do all the mincing for you. Cut the remaining 100g of venison loin into 1cm dice and put it in a bowl with all the minced meat.

Add a little oil to a frying pan and sauté the mushrooms and shallots with the herbs and spices until soft. Add the Madeira and port to the pan and reduce by one-third. Leave to cool.

Add the cooled mushroom and shallot mixture to the minced meat and cubed venison. Add the green peppercorns, pistachios and eggs and mix thoroughly. Leave to marinate overnight.

The next day, preheat the oven to 160°C/Fan 140°C/Gas 3. Warm a little oil in a frying pan and cook the black pudding for about 4 minutes on each side until crispy, then set aside.

Line a terrine mould or a cake tin with a capacity of about 1.4 litres with the caul fat, allowing it to overhang the sides. Add half of the terrine mixture, pushing it down as firmly as possible, then add the black pudding. Add the rest of the terrine mixture, then fold over the excess caul fat and press it down to remove any air. Place in the oven and cook for about 1 hour and 10 minutes. The core temperature should reach 63°C.

Remove from the oven and leave to cool, then press the terrine down with something heavy such as a couple of tins. Make sure you put a tray underneath as juices will come out. Leave it overnight in the fridge.

Serve with a chicory salad or a green salad with a sharp vinaigrette to cut through the richness of the pâté. The pâté keeps in the fridge for about 4 days.

CHAPTER FIVE

SWEET FINISH

Les desserts gourmands

Iced nougat with three melons & blueberry sauce

Nougat glacé aux trois melons et sauce aux myrtilles

Serves eight

Caramelised hazelnuts
80g caster sugar
80g hazelnuts

Nougat
6 free-range egg whites
250g caster sugar
375ml whipping cream,
    whipped
1 dessertspoon vanilla extract

Blueberry sauce
500g blueberries
100g caster sugar
Juice of 1 lemon

To serve
1 Charentais melon,
    1 Ogen melon and a
    thick slice of watermelon

When I want to make my wife Gisèle happy, this is the dessert I cook and it is truly wonderful. The nougat can be prepared in advance and kept in the freezer, ready to serve with fruit to cut through the richness. I'm suggesting melon and blueberries here, but this dessert is also good served with other fruit, such as raspberries and strawberries.

First make the caramelised hazelnuts. Oil a baking tray. Put the sugar in a heavy-based saucepan over a moderate heat and melt, stirring with a wooden spoon until it turns into a golden caramel. Add the nuts and continue to cook until the nuts are well coated and the caramel bubbles again. Pour the mixture on to the baking tray and leave to set. Once set, break the hazelnuts into large crumbs with a rolling pin and set aside.

Next, make the nougat. Line a 900g loaf tin with cling film. Place a bowl over a saucepan of simmering water, add the egg whites and sugar and whisk gently until the mixture is warm and the sugar has dissolved. Remove the bowl from the pan and whisk at full speed, until cold. The mixture should be smooth, yet firm. Fold in the whipped cream, vanilla and crushed caramelised nuts. Pour the mixture into the loaf tin and freeze for 24 hours.

For the sauce, blend the berries and sugar together until smooth. Press through a fine sieve into a bowl and add the lemon juice to taste. All soft fruit and berries can be made into sauces in this way – the natural sweetness of the fruit will determine how much or little sugar you add.

To assemble, turn out the iced nougat and slice it. Scoop the melons into little balls with a melon baller and divide them between your dishes. Add the sauce and slices of iced nougat to each serving and enjoy immediately.

Soufflé with chocolate sauce & macarons
Soufflé Lamberty

Serves six

For the moulds
50g butter, melted
20g caster sugar

Crème pâtissière
6 free-range egg yolks
85g caster sugar
60g flour
1 vanilla pod, seeds
    scraped out
500ml milk
1 tsp vanilla extract

Chocolate sauce
250ml milk
25g cocoa powder
125g dark chocolate
    (70% cocoa solids),
    broken up

Base
12 chocolate macarons or
    other chocolate biscuits,
    such as bourbons
20ml Crème de Cacao or
    liqueur of your choice

Soufflé
8 free-range egg whites
50g caster sugar

To finish
1 tbsp icing sugar

A very impressive dessert, this is my version of the classic Soufflé Lamberty. The original is made with chocolate macarons, but it works well with other chocolate biscuits, such as bourbons. There's some last-minute work, then you pop the soufflés in the oven and wait for the magic to happen. This really does have the wow factor.

Butter the insides of 4 soufflé moulds, 10–12cm in diameter, then dust them with sugar.

For the crème pâtissière, mix the egg yolks, sugar, flour and vanilla seeds together in a bowl. Put the milk in a pan with the scraped-out vanilla pod and the vanilla extract and bring to the boil. Then pour the milk mixture on to the egg yolk mixture in the bowl and whisk well. Tip everything back into the pan and bring back to the boil. Cook until the mixture has thickened, then push it through a sieve. Set aside and leave to cool slightly.

For the chocolate sauce, boil the milk with the cocoa powder and whisk in the chocolate. Set aside in a warm place for later.

Divide the macarons or biscuits between the moulds, breaking them up if necessary, and add a teaspoon of liqueur to each one. Preheat the oven to 200°C/Fan 180°C/Gas 6.

Whisk the egg whites with the 50g of sugar until stiff, then fold this into the crème pâtissière mixture. Divide the mixture between the moulds and level the top with a palette knife. Rub your thumb around the edge of each mould – this helps the soufflés to rise.

Bake for about 12 minutes until well risen. Dust with icing sugar and serve at once with the warm chocolate sauce.

Champagne jelly with citrus fruits & blackberries

Gelée de fruits au champagne

Serves six

2 oranges
2 pink grapefruits
250g caster sugar
2 pears
5 lemon verbena stalks
20 gelatine leaves,
    soaked in cold water
    for 5 minutes
750ml champagne
150g blackberries

A champagne jelly is a real treat but you could also make this with sparkling wine. It looks beautiful and is very refreshing. You can make one large jelly or individual ones and vary the fruit according to the season. Nice with some crisp biscuits.

First, segment the citrus fruit. Slice the top and bottom off an orange with a sharp knife, then cut away the skin, working from top to bottom and removing all the white pith as well as the skin. Then carefully insert the knife between the membranes to separate the segments and remove them. Repeat with the remaining citrus fruit and lay the segments on a cloth to dry.

Pour 400ml of water into a pan and add the caster sugar. Place over a medium heat and bring to a simmer, stirring until the sugar dissolves. Peel the pears, cut them in half and core, then add them to the syrup and cook until tender. Remove the pears and cut them into large dice, then set aside.

Drain and squeeze the gelatine leaves, then add them with the verbena to the syrup. Leave to infuse off the heat for about 5 minutes. Pour the mixture into a bowl, removing the verbena, and add the champagne. Place the bowl into a larger bowl filled with ice cubes and stir the jelly every now and then until it has thickened slightly.

Take a 1.5 litre jelly mould and add some of the fruit, then a few ladlefuls of jelly. Continue layering in the fruit and jelly, then cover and refrigerate for at least 12 hours.

To serve, dip the mould into warm water to loosen the jelly, then tip it out on to a serving dish.

Almond & raspberry frangipane tart
Tarte Amandine

Serves six to eight

Pastry
150g butter, softened
90g caster sugar
2 free-range eggs
pinch of salt
240g plain flour,
    plus extra for dusting
75g ground almonds

Almond cream
200g butter, softened
200g caster sugar
200g ground almonds
2 tbsp plain flour
4 free-range eggs
1 tbsp dark rum or Ratafia
    (fruit-based liqueur)

Jam and fruit
60g raspberry jam
250g raspberries

To serve
Icing sugar
Ice cream or chantilly cream
    (see p.171)

I adore almond puddings and this French version of a Bakewell tart is one of my favourites. It's rich and indulgent but there is some fruit in there as well! Raspberries work perfectly with almonds but cherries would also be good here.

For the pastry, mix the softened butter with the caster sugar until combined. Mix in the eggs, then add the salt, flour and ground almonds and bring everything together into a dough. You can do this by hand or in a food processor or stand mixer.

Wrap the pastry in cling film and chill it in the fridge for about 2 hours. Dust your work surface with flour, roll out the pastry and use it to line a tart tin or flan ring measuring about 24cm in diameter. Chill again until needed.

For the almond cream, whisk the butter and sugar until pale, then add the ground almonds and flour and whisk to combine. Whisk in the eggs, one at a time, then add the rum or Ratafia.

Preheat the oven to 180°C/Fan 160°C/Gas 4. Remove the tart case from the fridge and spread a thin layer of jam over the pastry. Add the almond cream and arrange the raspberries evenly on top.

Bake for about 45 minutes until the tart is golden and cooked through. Dust with icing sugar and serve warm with ice cream or cool with chantilly cream. Don't put this tart in the fridge.

Diplomat pudding
Crème diplomate

4 slices of stale bread
or leftover brioche
or croissants
4 slices of good-quality
bread, crusts removed
1 tbsp icing sugar,
for dusting
2 tbsp golden raisins
2 tbsp sultanas
60ml dark rum
150g caster sugar
6 free-range egg yolks
250ml milk
250ml single cream
Seeds from 1 vanilla pod
Butter, for greasing
Apricot jam, warmed,
to glaze

I love these little puddings when they are still warm but they are also good cold. They are an ideal way of using up any stale bread, brioche or croissants and are easy to make.

Preheat the oven to 180°C/Fan 160°C/Gas 4. Cut the bread, brioche or croissants into chunks and spread them evenly over a baking tray. Dust with icing sugar and toast in the oven for 5–10 minutes until crisp. Remove and turn the oven down to 140°C/Fan 120°C/Gas 1.

Place the raisins and sultanas in a saucepan and cover with cold water. Bring to the boil, then strain into a dish. Add the rum and leave the fruit to cool.

Mix the sugar and egg yolks together in a large bowl until light and fluffy. Mix the milk and cream together in a jug, then stir in the vanilla seeds and add them to the eggs and sugar. Pass this custard mixture through a sieve, then set aside.

Butter 4 ramekin dishes, about 10 x 8cm in size, and butter 4 pieces of foil large enough to cover each dish. Fill the dishes with the toasted bread and divide the fruit and rum mixture between them. Ladle the custard over the bread and fruit in each ramekin.

Cover the ramekins with the buttered foil and place them in a roasting tin. Add enough warm water to come about 2cm up the sides of the ramekins. Bake in the oven for about 30 minutes or until set.

Glaze the puddings with a little warmed apricot jam and enjoy them hot or cold.

Glazed melon
Melon glacé

1 Charentais melon,
　cut in half
50g caster sugar
400g fresh berries
　(strawberries, raspberries,
　blackcurrants, redcurrants,
　blueberries)
1 lemon verbena sprig,
　leaves finely sliced
1 mint sprig, leaves
　finely sliced
2 big scoops of lemon sorbet
150ml cold sparkling
　or sweet wine

*A super-quick dessert to make, this is refreshing and looks beautiful.
It's a perfect summer treat.*

Scoop out the seeds from the melon halves. With a sharp knife,
cut a thin slice off the base of each half so they sit steadily on
your plates.

Sprinkle the rim of each melon with sugar and caramelise with
a blowtorch. Repeat this a couple of times to get a nice golden
crust. If you don't have a blowtorch, brown the melon halves
under a hot grill.

Mix the berries with the lemon verbena and mint, then spoon
them into each melon half. Add a scoop of lemon sorbet on
each one and finally pour over some cold sparkling wine.

Serve immediately!

Sabayon with glazed chestnuts
Sabayon aux marrons glacés

Serves four

10 marrons glacés
8 free-range egg yolks
250g icing sugar
Seeds from 1 vanilla pod
300ml dry white wine
100ml Grand Marnier
    or brandy

*Marrons glacés – chestnuts that have been confited in sugar syrup –
are a real delicacy that we always have at Christmas. I love to serve
little nuggets of them in a bowl of light creamy sabayon. The choice
of liqueur is up to you and what you have available, or you could
also use a little sweet wine instead.*

Cut the marrons glacés into quarters and divide them
between your serving glasses.

Whisk the egg yolks with the sugar, vanilla seeds and wine
in a heatproof bowl. Place the bowl over a pan of simmering
water and whisk until the mixture is pale, lightly thickened
and the whisk leaves trails in the top.

Whisk in the Grand Marnier or brandy and continue to
whisk for about 2 minutes until frothy. Remove the bowl
from the pan and continue to whisk for another minute
until the mixture forms soft peaks. Divide the sabayon
between the glasses and serve at once.

Blackberry & apple mille-feuilles

Mille-feuilles aux mûres et pommes

Serves four

500g caster sugar
1 cinnamon stick
2 Cox's apples, peeled,
    quartered and cored
1 vanilla pod, split
200g blackberries
320g ready-rolled
    puff pastry
200g icing sugar
100g crème pâtissière
    (see p.238)
100ml double cream

Some classic French pastry skills on show for this fancy version of blackberry and apple pie. A bit of work but impressive and delicious.

Put the 500g of sugar in a pan with a litre of water and bring to the boil. Add the cinnamon stick and the apple quarters, then poach the apples until tender but not falling apart. Remove the apples and set them aside.

Add the vanilla pod to the poaching liquid. Add the berries and leave them to infuse in the liquid off the heat for about 20 minutes until cooled completely. Drain the blackberries, then put the poaching liquid back over the heat until it is reduced to a syrup. Leave to cool, then set aside.

Preheat the oven to 240°C/Fan 220°C/Gas 9. Roll the puff pastry out as thinly as you can. Sprinkle the pastry with some icing sugar, making sure it's evenly covered.

Put the pastry on a baking tray, cover it with a sheet of baking paper and place a wire rack on top – the rack should be just heavy enough to stop the pastry from bubbling up too much. Bake the pastry for about 5 minutes, then remove the wire rack and bake for another 5 minutes until golden brown. Leave the pastry to cool, then cut it into 12 equal rectangles.

Whip the crème pâtissière. Then whip the cream to a ribbon stage and fold in the crème pâtissière. Put the mixture in a piping bag. Pipe some of the cream mixture on to 4 of the pastry rectangles and add a couple of apple quarters to each one. Place another piece of pastry on top of the apples. Pipe on a little more cream and add some blackberries and then top with another piece of pastry and dust with icing sugar. Serve the mille-feuilles with the blackberry syrup.

Roast plums, almonds & whisky

Prunes rôties, amandes et whisky

Serves four

2 tbsp caster sugar
2 tbsp unsalted butter
8 plums, halved and
    stones removed
2 tbsp flaked or
    nibbed almonds
4 tbsp whisky
Juice of ½ lemon

Chantilly cream
240ml whipping cream
2 tbsp icing sugar

Puff pastry crisps (optional)
2 tbsp caster sugar
320g all-butter puff pastry

This simple fruit dessert can also be made with apricots, peaches or nectarines, and if you're not a whisky fan, dark rum or brandy are good alternatives. The puff pastry crisps are optional but they do provide a lovely crunch that complements the fruit.

Melt the sugar and butter in a pan, add the plums and allow them to colour on both sides. Take care not to let the butter and sugar burn. Add the almonds, whisky and lemon juice and continue to cook until the plums are tender but not mushy.

For the chantilly cream, whip the cream until fluffy, but don't over whip it or you will make butter! Stir in the sugar.

For the pastry crisps, if using, preheat the oven to 200°C/Fan 180°C/Gas 6. Sprinkle your work surface with caster sugar and roll out the pastry as thinly as you can. Place it on a baking tray and cover with greaseproof paper and another baking tray to keep the pastry from bubbling up too much.

Bake for 25 minutes, then remove the tray and paper. Turn the heat up to 220°C/Fan 200°C/Gas 7 and cook the pastry for about another 15 minutes until golden.

Remove the pastry from the oven and while it is still hot, cut out squares measuring about 7 x 7cm, then set them aside to cool.

Serve the plums and sauce with the chantilly cream and puff pastry crisps.

Coffee cream pots
Petits pots de crème au café

150g caster sugar
500ml milk
40g coffee beans,
    lightly crushed
6 free-range egg yolks
5 gelatine leaves (8g),
    soaked in cold water
500ml whipping cream
2 tbsp cocoa powder,
    to serve

Chantilly cream
150ml whipping cream
Seeds from ½ vanilla pod
1 tbsp icing sugar

For lovers of latte or creamy milky coffee, this is the ultimate dessert. I like serving these in little retro-style glasses – and if they're all different it just adds to the fun. The coffee pots can be made in advance and left to chill and set overnight, then finished off with a little chantilly cream and a dusting of cocoa powder just before serving.

Put 75g of the sugar in a pan and place over a medium heat until it has turned a dark caramel. Remove the pan from the heat and pour the milk into the caramel, making sure that it does not boil over. Then put the pan back over the heat and bring to the boil, stirring to blend the milk and caramel.

Remove the pan from the heat and stir in the lightly crushed coffee beans. Cover and leave to infuse for about 20 minutes, then pass the mixture through a fine sieve.

Whisk the egg yolks in a bowl with the rest of the sugar until pale. Add the boiled milk and caramel to the egg mixture and stir well to combine. Pour the mixture into a pan and place over the heat. Keep stirring constantly until the mixture has thickened and coats the back of a spoon, then immediately take the pan off the heat.

Squeeze the excess water out of the gelatine leaves and add them to the mixture. Then place the pan over a bowl of iced water to cool. Once the mixture has cooled a little, but not set, pass it through a fine sieve. Whip the cream to soft peaks and stir it into the mixture. Pour into little pots and chill in the fridge overnight.

Before serving, make the chantilly cream. Whip the cream with the vanilla seeds and the icing sugar until stiff. Spoon or pipe on top of the pots, then dust with cocoa powder.

Souffléd pancakes with oranges & Grand Marnier

Crêpes soufflées à l'orange et Grand Marnier

Serves four

4 oranges
250g crème pâtissière
   (see p.238)
6 free-range egg whites
Pinch of sugar
50ml Grand Marnier
20g icing sugar,
   for dusting

Pancakes
1 free-range egg
75g plain flour
1 tbsp caster sugar
Pinch of salt
210ml milk
1 tbsp clarified butter
   (see p.234)

This show-stopping dessert was one of my Uncle Michel's favourites.

First make the pancake batter. Beat the egg in a bowl, then whisk in the flour a little at a time. Add the sugar and salt and mix well with a whisk. Stir in the milk to make a smooth batter, then leave it to rest in a cool place for at least an hour. To cook, brush a frying pan or crêpe pan with a little of the clarified butter and heat. Ladle in less than a quarter of the batter and cook the pancake for 1 or 2 minutes on each side, turning it with a palette knife. You should get 4 or 5 pancakes.

Segment 2 of the oranges (see page 86) and squeeze all the membranes into a pan to extract any juice. Add the juice of the other 2 oranges to the pan. Place over a low heat and reduce by half, then strain into a bowl and set aside at room temperature.

Put the crème pâtissière in a bowl, place it over a pan of simmering water and heat gently. Meanwhile, beat the egg whites with a pinch of sugar until they form soft peaks. Take the crème pâtissière off the heat, whisk in the Grand Marnier and beat briefly, then add one-third of the egg whites. Mix well, then carefully fold in the rest of the egg whites with a spatula. Preheat the oven to 240°C/Fan 220°C/Gas 9.

Lay a pancake on a board and spoon a quarter of the crème pâtissière mix over one half. Add a few orange segments, then fold the pancake over and press down gently to seal the edges. Repeat with the remaining pancakes, crème pâtissière mix and orange segments. Put the filled pancakes on a lightly greased baking tray and bake in the preheated oven for 2–5 minutes. Remove and dust them generously with icing sugar, then place under a hot grill for 4–5 minutes, so that the sugar melts and becomes partly caramelised. To serve, slide each pancake on to a plate. Pour some of the reduced orange juice around each one and add a few orange segments. Serve at once.

Strawberry & Maraschino cream with fresh strawberries

Mousse de fraises au Marasquin et fraises

Serves six

450g strawberries, hulled
50g caster sugar, plus 2 tbsp
250g crème pâtissière
    (see p.238)
4 tbsp Maraschino liqueur
250ml soured cream
50ml whipping cream,
    whipped to soft peaks

To serve
Crisp biscuits

A French version of strawberries and cream with a touch of luxury from the liqueur, this is quick to make and delicious to eat.

Put 250g of the strawberries in a blender with the 50g of sugar and blitz to form a purée. Pass the purée through a fine strainer into a bowl and discard the seeds.

Cut the remaining strawberries into halves or into quarters if large. Heat the 2 tablespoons of sugar with 100ml of water and bring to the boil, then add the strawberries and cook to make a compote. Leave to cool.

Whisk the crème pâtissière, then slowly add the liqueur. Add the soured cream and whisk, then add the strawberry purée and whisk until completely amalgamated. Fold the whipped cream into the mixture.

Divide the Maraschino cream between your bowls and top with some strawberry compote. Serve with crisp biscuits or even a scoop of strawberry ice cream.

Dark chocolate tart with caramelised bananas

Tarte au chocolat noir et bananes caramelisées

Serves six

200ml whipping cream
3 tbsp whole milk
200g dark chocolate
(70% cocoa solids),
broken up
2 medium free-range eggs
1 x 25cm precooked sweet
shortcrust pastry case
(see p.242)
1 tbsp cocoa powder,
for dusting

Caramelised bananas
100g caster sugar
3 bananas, cut into chunks
100g unsalted butter
20ml dark rum

Chocolate, bananas and rum – what's not to like? This is a great combination. For best results, use bananas that are not too ripe and I find dark chocolate works best with the sweetness of the bananas. A perfect dessert to enjoy in winter when good fresh berries are scarce.

Pour the cream and milk into a saucepan. Stir and bring to the boil over a medium heat. Remove the pan from the heat, add the pieces of chocolate, then stir until the chocolate has melted completely. Allow to cool. Preheat the oven to 150°C/ Fan 130°C/Gas 2.

Beat the eggs in a bowl. When the chocolate mixture has cooled, whisk in the beaten eggs until they are completely amalgamated. Pour the mixture into the pastry case and smooth the top with a spatula. Bake for 15–20 minutes.

Meanwhile, prepare the bananas. Heat a frying pan, add the sugar and allow it to melt to a golden caramel. Then add the bananas and turn them in the sugar until caramelised. When the caramel turns dark, add the butter and stir until melted, then add the dark rum. Continue to cook until the liquid is reduced by half and is a nice syrupy consistency. Remove from the heat and set aside.

Allow the tart to cool slightly and serve warm or at room temperature. Sprinkle with cocoa powder and serve with the warm caramelised bananas on top of the tart. Do not refrigerate the tart.

Pears in red wine
Poires au vin rouge

Serves six

6 slightly firm pears
   (Conference, Williams
   or Comice)
1 bottle of red wine
   (Pinot or Gamay)
200g caster sugar
1 cinnamon stick
1 vanilla pod, split
6 black peppercorns
1 strip of orange peel
4 tbsp crème de cassis

To serve
Crème fraiche

I never tire of this one and the longer you steep the pears in the wine, the darker and more delicious they become. Nice with a dollop of crème fraiche, but I also enjoy these pears with a slice of good blue cheese.

Peel and core the pears from the base, taking care to leave the stalks in place.

Put all the remaining ingredients, except the crème de cassis, into a pan and bring to the boil. Add the pears, making sure they are submerged in the liquid, and cover with a piece of greaseproof paper. Simmer for 20 minutes or until tender, then carefully tip everything into a bowl and leave to cool. Add the crème de cassis and chill in the fridge overnight.

If you would like a thicker syrup, decant the liquid into a pan and boil until it is reduced by a third. Serve the pears with the syrup and some crème fraiche.

Chocolate mousse
Mousse au chocolat

Serves six to eight

220g dark chocolate
(minimum 70% cocoa
solids), broken up
1 tbsp butter
8 free-range eggs
2 tbsp caster sugar
Coarse sea salt (optional)

To serve (optional)
Raspberries
Crème fraiche

There are so many recipes for chocolate mousse, but this is the one I like the most. It came from my Grandma Roux and has the addition of a little butter to make it even more indulgent. She was from Normandy and so added butter and cream to everything!

Put the broken-up chocolate and the butter in a heatproof bowl with 2 tablespoons of water and place the bowl over a pan of simmering water. Make sure the bottom of the bowl doesn't touch the water. Allow the chocolate to melt slowly and don't let it overheat. Once the chocolate has melted, set it aside to cool slightly.

Separate the eggs. Make sure you put the whites into a scrupulously clean bowl with no trace of fat or they won't whisk properly. Whisk the egg yolks into the melted chocolate and then set aside.

Add the sugar to the egg whites and beat until stiff. Fold them into the chocolate, a little at a time. I like to add just a pinch of coarse sea salt to bring out the flavour of the chocolate, but that's up to you.

Spoon into small bowls or cups and chill for a couple of hours before serving. Add raspberries and crème fraiche if you like.

Sweet choux buns with caramel & chocolate sauce

Choux au caramel et sauce au chocolat

Choux buns
250ml milk
100g butter, diced
½ tsp fine salt
1 tsp sugar
150g plain flour, sifted
4 medium free-range eggs

Chantilly cream
240ml whipping cream
2 tbsp icing sugar

To serve
250g caster sugar,
    for the caramel
Chocolate sauce (see p.157)

Choux pastry is so versatile and a great technique to master. You can fill these little buns with anything and everything, such as chocolate mousse, praline or jam – the choice is yours. Have fun!

Preheat the oven to 220°C/Fan 200°C/Gas 7. Put the milk, butter, salt and sugar in a saucepan with 125ml of water and bring to the boil. Take the pan off the heat and quickly add the flour, then put the pan back over the heat and stir with a spatula. Continue to beat and cook over a medium heat for a couple of minutes until the paste comes away from the sides of the pan. Tip the paste into a bowl, then immediately beat in the eggs, one at the time, with a spatula and stir well until the paste is beautifully smooth.

Take a piping bag and fit a plain 1cm nozzle. Line a baking tray with baking parchment. Fill the piping bag with the choux paste and pipe out round ball shapes, about 2–2.5cm in diameter, on to the baking tray. You should get about 16–20.

Bake the choux buns for about 10 minutes, until brown and risen. Then lower the heat to 180°C/Fan 160°C/Gas 4 and cook for about 20 minutes longer, until crisp and dry. Leave to cool before filling.

For the chantilly cream, whip the cream until fluffy, but don't over whip it. Stir in the sugar and put the mixture in a piping bag. Make a hole with a knife in the side of each choux bun and fill with chantilly cream.

For the caramel, put the 250g of caster sugar in a pan over a high heat and cook until golden brown, stirring occasionally. Remove from the heat and cool briefly, then very, very carefully dip the tops of the choux buns in the caramel. It will be hot! Serve immediately with chocolate sauce.

CHAPTER SIX

FAMILY CELEBRATIONS AT HOME

Dîners festifs en famille

SPRING CELEBRATIONS

Choux buns filled with pea mousse (canapé)
Choux à la mousse de petits pois

Grilled asparagus with cobnuts
Asperges grillées aux noisettes

Provence fish stew with aioli sauce
Bourride Sétoise

Baked bomb Alaska with vanilla ice cream & rhubarb coulis
Omelette Norvégienne et coulis à la rhubarbe

Choux buns filled with pea mousse (canapé)

Choux à la mousse de petits pois

Serves six (three each)

Choux buns
150ml whole milk
50g butter, diced
½ tsp fine salt
75g flour, sifted
2 free-range eggs
1 tbsp sunflower seeds

Pea mousse
150g frozen peas
75g whole milk
25ml olive oil
½ tsp Maldon sea salt
½ tsp caster sugar
2 gelatine leaves
Black pepper

To garnish
Handful of pea shoots

Pea mousse is simple to make, but you could also use different fillings for these tasty little choux buns, such as smoked salmon.

Make the pea mousse the day before you want to serve the buns. Put the peas in a blender or a powerful food processor with the milk and oil, then add the salt, sugar and a grinding of pepper. Start blending slowly, then after about 5 minutes increase the speed and continue until you have a smooth purée. It will take around 15 minutes to get a really smooth result.

Soak the gelatine in cold water, then drain and squeeze out the excess water. Heat 2 tablespoons of the purée and melt the gelatine into it. Add this to the rest of the purée and whisk it through. Place the mousse in the fridge overnight.

For the choux buns, put the milk, butter and salt in a pan with 75ml of water and bring to the boil. Take the pan off the heat, quickly add the flour and beat vigorously until the mixture comes together as a smooth paste. Put the pan back over the heat and continue to beat for 2 or 3 minutes. Pour the mixture into a bowl and beat in the eggs one at a time, stirring well until the mixture is smooth.

Line a baking tray with baking parchment. Cut a hole about 2cm wide in your piping bag. Fill the piping bag with the choux paste and pipe out round ball shapes, about 2.5cm in diameter, on to the baking tray. Sprinkle with the sunflower seeds. Bake the buns at 220°C/Fan 200°C/Gas 7 for about 20 minutes until well risen and golden. Open the oven door to let out the steam, then close the door and lower the heat to 180°C/Fan 160°C/Gas 4. Cook the choux buns for about 10 more minutes – they should be dry and crisp. Leave to cool before filling.

Take the mousse out of the fridge and whisk it, then put it into a piping bag. Make a hole with a knife in the side of each choux bun and fill them with the pea mousse. Serve immediately.

Grilled asparagus with cobnuts
Asperges grillées aux noisettes

Serves six

2 small red onions,
sliced into very fine rings
36 green asparagus spears
4 tbsp olive oil
60g peeled cobnuts
or hazelnuts
6 tbsp hazelnut oil
2 tbsp red wine vinegar
Juice of ½ lemon
Salt and black pepper

When asparagus is in season, I like to eat as much of it as I can, then forget about it for the rest of the year. This dish is best made with medium-sized green asparagus and is perfect as a simple starter or to serve with grilled fish. I like cobnuts – a nod to Kent where I was born and where they grow in abundance – or you can use hazelnuts.

First, put the red onion rings in a bowl of cold water and leave them to soak for about 20 minutes to remove any harshness. Take the asparagus spears and bend the stalk of each one until it snaps, then discard the woody ends. Peel the stalks if you think it's necessary.

Toss the spears in the olive oil until they are coated all over, then season with a little salt and pepper. Place the spears on a griddle pan or barbecue and cook on all sides until charred and tender. This should take about 5 minutes – the asparagus should still have a little bite to it.

Put the cobnuts or hazelnuts in a dry pan and toast them over a medium heat until brown. Keep the nuts moving or they will burn quite easily. Once the nuts are well toasted, crush them and add the hazelnut oil and vinegar. Season well with salt, pepper and lemon juice.

Drizzle some of the hazelnut dressing over the asparagus and scatter the drained onion rings on top.

Provence fish stew
with aioli sauce
Bourride Sétoise

Serves six

2 tbsp olive oil
2 carrots, sliced
1 leek, sliced
300g small new
    potatoes, sliced
200ml dry white wine
1 pinch of saffron
500ml fish stock
3 bay leaves
1kg monkfish, skinned and
    cut into small pieces
6 langoustines or
    large prawns
120g aioli (see p.233)
Chopped flatleaf parsley
Salt and black pepper

There are many versions of this recipe but this is mine and I'm sticking by it. I use monkfish, which is traditional, and I like to add some langoustine or prawns to make the dish even more special. Stir in some aioli or serve it on the side for your friends to help themselves if they are worried about the strength of the garlic!

Heat the oil in a sauté pan, add the carrots, leek and potatoes, then sweat until tender. Season with salt and pepper. Add the wine and saffron and deglaze the pan, scraping up any sticky bits. Pour in the stock, bring to the boil and add the bay leaves.

Add the pieces of monkfish, partially cover the pan with a lid and simmer for 3–4 minutes, then add the langoustines or prawns. Once the fish and shellfish are cooked, lift them out with a slotted spoon and place in warm bowls.

Put the pan of vegetables and stock back over the heat and bring to the boil. Stir in the aioli, then pour the contents of the pan over the fish and shellfish in the bowls. Sprinkle with chopped parsley and serve.

Baked bomb Alaska with vanilla ice cream & rhubarb coulis
Omelette Norvégienne et coulis à la rhubarbe

Serves six

Sponge base
150g unsalted butter
150g caster sugar
4 free-range eggs
150g self-raising flour

Rhubarb coulis
350g rhubarb,
　trimmed and tough
　strings removed
50g caster sugar
1 tsp ground ginger
½ vanilla pod,
　seeds scraped out
Juice of 1 lemon

Italian meringue
310g caster sugar
60g liquid glucose
8 egg whites

To finish
300g vanilla ice cream
200g fresh strawberries
100g icing sugar

A classic all over the world, this desssert never fails to impress.

Preheat the oven to 200°C/Fan 180°C/Gas 6. Grease a 20 x 30cm baking tray and line it with baking parchment. Cream the butter and sugar in a bowl until pale. Beat in the eggs, one at a time, then gently fold in the flour. Spread the mixture in the baking tray and bake for 20–25 minutes. Remove and leave to cool to room temperature on a rack.

For the rhubarb coulis, put the rhubarb, sugar, ginger, vanilla pod and seeds and the lemon juice in a pan with 100ml of water. Heat gently until the rhubarb starts breaking down. Remove the vanilla pod, put 6 tablespoons of rhubarb aside, then blend the rest of the rhubarb until smooth. Strain through a sieve and chill in the fridge until needed.

For the Italian meringue, mix the sugar and glucose in a pan with 70ml of water. Bring to the boil and cook until the syrup reaches 121°C on a sugar thermometer. Meanwhile, beat the egg whites to stiff peaks with an electric whisk. Pour the hot syrup on to the egg whites in a continuous thin stream while still beating. Keep beating until the meringue has cooled, then leave to cool completely.

To assemble, preheat the oven to 220°C/Fan 200°C/Gas 7. Line a baking tray with greaseproof paper. Cut the sponge into 6 circles measuring about 7cm in diameter and place them on the lined tray. Add a spoonful of the reserved rhubarb, then a scoop of vanilla ice cream to each sponge circle.

Fill a piping bag with the meringue and pipe it around the sponge and over the ice cream, making sure everything is covered. Immediately put the Alaskas in the oven and bake for 5–8 minutes until the meringue is golden brown. Spread some coulis on each plate and place a baked Alaska on top. Garnish with strawberries and dust with icing sugar, then serve at once.

SUMMER CELEBRATIONS

Smoked trout & salmon mousse tartlets (canapé)
Croustillant à la mousse de truite fumée et saumon

Chilled soup with radish tops & nettles
Velouté glacé de fanes de radis et orties

Barbecued flank steak & bulgur salad
Steak au barbecue et salade de boulgour

Floating islands with raspberry compote
Iles flottantes et compote de framboises

Smoked trout & salmon mousse tartlets (canapé)

Croustillant à la mousse de truite fumée et saumon

Serves six

50g smoked trout
70g smoked salmon
Juice of 1 lemon
1 pinch of cayenne pepper
125ml double cream
Vegetable oil, for greasing
3 sheets of brick pastry
   (feuille de brick)
1 free-range egg yolk
Paprika
Salt

A creamy fish mousse served in crisp brick pastry shells, these make an excellent start to a summer menu. Brick pastry is available online and in some supermarkets.

Put the smoked trout and 50g of the smoked salmon into a blender with the lemon juice and cayenne pepper. Season with salt, then blend until smooth. Pass the mixture through a fine sieve, then refrigerate.

Whip the cream to soft peaks and gently fold the cream into the salmon and trout mixture. Dice the remaining 20g of smoked salmon and add it to the mixture. Preheat the oven to 180°C/Fan 160°C/Gas 4.

Grease 6 small tartlet moulds or mince pie tins with vegetable oil. Cut the brick pastry into 6 rounds measuring about 6cm in diameter and use them to line the moulds. Bake in the oven for about 5 minutes until crisp.

Put the mousse into a piping bag and fill the tartlets.
Dust with paprika, then serve.

Chilled soup with radish tops & nettles

Velouté glacé de fanes de radis et orties

Serves six

500g leeks,
   white parts only
100g nettles
1 bunch of radishes
1 tbsp olive oil
1 garlic clove, chopped
100g long-grain rice
1 litre vegetable stock

To garnish
200g different
   coloured radishes
1 tbsp white balsamic vinegar
Salt and black pepper

If you live in the countryside, finding nettles should be easy. Wear rubber gloves so you don't get stung and pick the nettles in unpolluted areas. Choose the smaller leaves which have a lovely sorrel-like taste. If you can't find good nettles, use sorrel or watercress for this soup.

Cut the leek in half lengthways and then slice it into very fine semi-circles and wash well. Rinse the nettles in warm water, then drain. Separate the leaves from the radishes and wash them. Set the radishes aside to use for the garnish.

Heat the oil in a pan and add the leek and garlic. Cook gently over a medium heat, then add the rice, radish leaves and nettles and sweat briefly. Add the vegetable stock, bring to the boil and cook for 45–50 minutes over a low heat. Blend the soup and season with salt and pepper. Leave to cool, then refrigerate.

For the garnish, cut some of the radishes into rounds and slice the rest thinly on a mandolin or with a peeler. Put the thin slices into iced water to crisp up.

Bring a pan of salted water to the boil, add the round radish slices and cook for one minute. Remove and season with salt, pepper and balsamic vinegar, then leave to chill in the fridge until ready to serve.

Serve the chilled soup in bowls. Drain the thinly sliced radishes, season them with salt and pepper and add them to the bowls. Top with the pickled radishes and drizzle some olive oil over each serving.

Barbecued flank steak & bulgur salad
Steak au barbecue et salade de boulgour

6 flank steaks
(about 200g each),
at room temperature
3 tbsp Dijon mustard
Salt and black pepper

Bulgur salad
200g bulgur wheat
1 litre just-boiled water
6 tomatoes, peeled,
deseeded and diced
300g broad beans, blanched
and outer skins removed
2 spring onions, sliced
2 handfuls of chopped
parsley leaves
2 handfuls of chopped
mint leaves
Handful of basil leaves,
roughly chopped
20 pitted black olives
250g feta cheese, crumbled
Zest and juice of 2 lemons
3–4 tbsp olive oil

Flank steak is much loved in France for its flavour, and it's cheaper than many steak cuts. I do recommend cooking it rare, though, as it can be tough if overcooked. The smoky barbecue flavour is great here, but you can also cook this on a griddle pan indoors. The salad is colourful, easy to make and is a lovely summery accompaniment.

For the salad, put the bulgur wheat in a heatproof bowl and pour the boiling water over it. Cover tightly with cling film and leave it to steam for 15 minutes until tender. Strain to drain off any excess water, then tip the bulgur back into the bowl and set it aside to cool.

Once the bulgur is cool, add the diced tomatoes, broad beans, spring onions, herbs, olives, feta and the lemon zest and juice. Season with salt and pepper and a drizzle of olive oil.

Heat a griddle or barbecue and brush the steaks with the mustard. Season with salt and pepper and place them directly on the grill. Cook for 3 minutes on each side for rare meat, or for 5 minutes on each side for medium rare. Leave the steak to rest for about 5 minutes, then slice and serve with the salad.

Floating islands with raspberry compote

Iles flottantes et compote de framboises

Serves six

Raspberry compote
500g raspberries
100g sugar, or to taste

Crème anglaise
500ml milk
1 vanilla pod, split
6 free-range egg yolks
120g caster sugar

Meringue
6 free-range egg whites
150g caster sugar,
    plus 2 tbsp

Caramel
200g caster sugar

A family favourite and a real French classic, this is a perfect summer dessert served with seasonal fruit.

To make the compote, tip the berries into a pan and sprinkle with sugar to taste. Add a little water and simmer until the berries are tender.

To make the crème anglaise, bring the milk to the boil with the vanilla pod. Take the pan off the heat, cover and leave to infuse for 10 minutes. Beat the egg yolks with the sugar until thick and creamy. Bring the milk back to the boil and pour it on to the egg yolk mixture, while whisking continuously. Pour the mixture back into the pan and cook over a low heat, stirring continuously with a spatula, until the custard thickens slightly. It must not boil at this stage, or it will scramble.

For the meringue, beat the egg whites with a whisk until frothy, then add the 150g of caster sugar. Continue to whisk until the meringue is firm and smooth.

Bring a large pan of water, sweetened with the 2 tablespoons of caster sugar, to simmering point. Using a big spoon dipped in cold water, scoop out a big island of meringue and plunge the spoon into the simmering water. The island will come off the spoon. Leave it to poach, flipping it over after 3–4 minutes to cook on the other side. Once cooked, gently take the island out of the liquid with a slotted spoon and place it on a rack to cool and drain. Continue until you've used all the mixture.

To make the caramel, heat the 200g of caster sugar in a heavy-based pan until it is liquid and golden. To serve, place some compote in each bowl, followed by some crème anglaise, then a meringue island. Drizzle over the caramel and serve at once.

AUTUMN CELEBRATIONS

Pickled rock oysters (canapé)
Huîtres sauce aigre-douce

Rabbit & pork terrine
Terrine de lapin et porc

Venison stew with chestnuts, apricots & potatoes dauphinoise
Ragoût de chevreuil aux châtaignes et abricots, gratin dauphinois

Poached pears with chocolate & almond sauce
Poires pochées et sa sauce chocolat/amandes

Pickled rock oysters (canapé)

Huîtres sauce aigre-douce

15g caster sugar
150ml sherry vinegar
12 oysters
½ cucumber
1 banana shallot,
 finely diced
2 dill sprigs, chopped
Olive oil

Oysters always add a celebratory touch to a special meal. I like to use small oysters for this canapé and the pickling liquor works well with their salty flavour. If serving this as a starter, up the number of oysters.

Put the sugar in a pan with 20ml of water and bring the water to the boil, then take the pan off the heat. Chill, then stir in the sherry vinegar and set aside.

Open the oysters and remove the meat, reserving the shells. Drop the oysters into the pickle mixture and leave them for 20 minutes, then drain.

Meanwhile, peel the cucumber and cut it into small dice, about 5mm in size. Add the shallot and season with salt and pepper, then add half the chopped dill.

Clean the oyster shells and dry them. Divide the cucumber mixture between the shells, add the oysters and drizzle a little olive oil on top. Serve garnished with the rest of the dill.

Rabbit & pork terrine
Terrine de lapin et porc

Serves six

1 farmed rabbit, jointed
500g green ham hock
    or salted belly pork
500g carrots, chopped
350g celery, chopped
1 medium onion,
    finely chopped
1 garlic clove,
    finely chopped
1 thyme sprig
2 bay leaves
1 rosemary sprig
1 bottle of dry white wine
50g chives, chopped
Salt and black pepper

To garnish
100g piccalilli (see p.232 or
    use shop-bought piccalilli)

This is a simple terrine to make, but it does need to be prepared at least a day in advance, as the meat takes a while to cook and the terrine needs to be left to set overnight. You could use wild rabbit if you have some, but I find the flavour a bit too strong for this recipe. The sweet and sour piccalilli is a perfect accompaniment.

You will need a terrine dish, measuring about 24 x 8cm, or you could use a loaf tin.

Put the rabbit and ham hock or belly pork in a casserole dish with the chopped carrots, celery, onion, garlic and herbs, then season with salt and pepper. Add the wine and enough water to cover the meat and vegetables, then put a lid on the dish and cook for 2 hours in a low oven (120°C/Fan 100°C/Gas ½). Remove and leave to cool.

When everything is cool enough to handle, pick the rabbit meat off the bones and shred the pork. Set the meat aside.

Strain the cooking liquor and boil it in a pan on the hob until it has reduced to about 500–600ml. Pour the reduced liquor into a bowl, then add the rabbit and pork meat and the chopped chives. Pour everything into the terrine dish and cover with a lid or foil, then leave in the fridge overnight to set.

The next day, remove the terrine from the dish and cut into slices. Serve with piccalilli and salad.

Venison stew with chestnuts, apricots & potatoes dauphinoise

Ragoût de chevreuil aux châtaignes et abricots, gratin dauphinois

Serves six

1kg venison shoulder
   or neck, cut into cubes
   about 4 x 4cm
2 tbsp vegetable oil
1 medium onion, finely diced
1 carrot, finely diced
2 celery sticks, strings
   removed, finely diced
2 tbsp flour
1 tbsp tomato paste
4 juniper berries, chopped
125ml dry white wine
50ml chestnut liqueur
   or brandy
1 litre veal or beef stock
6 large dried apricots, halved
18 cooked chestnuts, halved
Salt and black pepper

Potatoes dauphinoise
2 garlic cloves, cut in half
750g potatoes, cut into
   slices about 2mm thick
500ml whipping cream
Grating of nutmeg
Salt and black pepper

You can't get more French than this combination of a beautiful slow-cooked stew and a creamy dauphinoise. Just right for a special autumn occasion. I like to use shoulder or neck for this stew, as it is cheaper than loin and more flavourful. As with all stews, this is best made the day before you want to eat it.

Season the venison with salt and pepper. Heat a tablespoon of the oil in a flameproof casserole dish, about 26–28cm in diameter, and brown the meat all over. It's best to do this in batches so you don't overcrowd the pan. Transfer each batch of browned meat to a colander set over a bowl to catch the juices.

Add a little more oil to the casserole dish and lightly brown the vegetables. Put the venison back in the dish with the vegetables, then add the flour, tomato paste and juniper berries. Season with salt and pepper. Cook for 2–3 minutes, add the wine and the liqueur or brandy, then let it bubble up and reduce. Simmer for 5 minutes, then add any venison juices to the dish.

Pour in the stock and bring to the boil. Cover the pan and leave to simmer for about 2 hours until the meat is tender. Add the apricots and chestnuts and cook until they are warmed through, then serve with the potatoes dauphinoise.

Potatoes dauphinoise

Preheat the oven to 200°C/Fan 180°C/Gas 6. Rub the inside of an ovenproof dish with the cut garlic. Mix the potatoes with the cream and season with salt, pepper and nutmeg, then transfer to the dish and cover with foil. Bake for 30 minutes, then remove the foil and cook for a further 20 minutes.

Poached pears with chocolate & almond sauce

Poires pochées et sa sauce chocolat/amandes

Serves six

450g caster sugar
1 vanilla pod, split and
    seeds scraped out
6 pears (William or similar)

Chocolate & almond sauce
90g unsweetened
    cocoa powder
180g caster sugar
45g unsalted butter
60g dark chocolate (70%
    cocoa solids), broken up
90g almonds, toasted
    and chopped

To serve
Whipped cream

Poached fruit is a very popular dessert in France – and in the Roux household. Anything with chocolate goes down particularly well with my young grandson!

Put the sugar, scraped vanilla pod and seeds in a pan with 700ml of water and bring to the boil.

Peel the pears. Remove the core from the base of each one, keeping the pears whole, then place them in the syrup and turn the heat down to a simmer. Cover with a piece of greaseproof paper and cook until a knife pierces a pear easily – the exact time will depend on the ripeness of the pear. Leave the pears to cool slightly in the syrup while you make the sauce.

For the sauce, put the cocoa powder and sugar in a pan with 240ml of water. Bring to the boil while whisking vigorously. Take the pan off the heat and whisk in the butter and chocolate, then add the almonds. Serve warm with the poached pears and whipped cream.

WINTER CELEBRATIONS

Smoked eel, beetroot & horseradish cream (canapé)
Anguille fumée, betterave et crème de raifort

Creamy mussels flavoured with curry
Mouclade d'Aunis

Pork tenderloin with Madeira sauce, salt-baked
celeriac & roast shallots
Filet de porc, sauce Madère, céleri-rave au sel et échalotes rôties

Caramelised apple pudding, toffee sauce
& Chantilly mascarpone
*Gâteau de pommes caramélisées, sauce au caramel
et Chantilly au mascarpone*

Smoked eel, beetroot & horseradish cream (canapé)

Anguille fumée, betterave et crème de raifort

Serves six

200ml sherry vinegar
2 star anise
6 pink peppercorns
150g small to medium
    raw beetroots, peeled
100ml double cream
15g creamed horseradish
150g smoked eel
Handful of pea shoots,
    to garnish
Grated horseradish (optional)

Quick and simple to make, this is an ideal canapé to serve at the start of a winter feast. Make sure you buy your eel from a reputable and sustainable source – if you don't like eel, smoked trout works well.

Put the sherry vinegar, star anise and peppercorns into a pan with 400ml of water and bring to the boil. Add the beetroots, cover the pan and cook them until soft. This will take about 25 minutes, depending on the size of the beetroots. Drain and set the beetroots aside to cool.

Whip the double cream until it forms soft peaks and then stir in the creamed horseradish. Slice the eel into bite-sized pieces.

Cut the beetroots into thin slices and arrange them on a serving dish. Add a spoonful of the horseradish and cream mixture to each slice and top with a piece of eel.

Garnish with pea shoots and serve at once. For an extra kick, you could grate some horseradish over each serving.

Creamy mussels flavoured with curry
Mouclade d'Aunis

Serves six

2kg mussels
Olive oil
1 onion, coarsely chopped
2 garlic cloves, crushed
1 thyme sprig
Parsley stalks
300ml dry white wine
1 tbsp butter
2 shallots, finely chopped
2 tsp mild curry powder
400ml double cream
Handful of chopped chervil
Handful of chopped
    coriander
Handful of chopped chives
Salt and black pepper

Mussels are cheap, plentiful and sustainable and this way of serving them in a curry-flavoured sauce was one of my dad's favourite dishes. He would eat big bowlfuls of this with great enthusiasm.

Wash and scrub the mussels in plenty of cold water, discarding any that are open or broken.

Heat a large pan with a splash of olive oil, then add the onion, garlic, thyme and parsley stalks.

Add the mussels and white wine, cover the pan and cook for 3 minutes. Remove the lid and shake the pan to toss the mussels around. Cover again and continue to cook until the mussels have opened.

Pour the contents of the pan into a colander set over a bowl to collect the juices. Strain the juices through a sieve lined with a muslin cloth. Pick the flesh from the mussels and set aside, discarding any mussels that haven't opened.

Melt the butter in another pan, add the shallots and sweat until they are soft, but not coloured. Add the curry powder and continue to cook for a further 3 minutes, then add the mussel cooking juices. Boil until reduced by half, then add the cream and boil again until the sauce has reduced and thickened.

Check the seasoning and fold in the mussels, then add the chopped herbs. Serve immediately – do not boil or the mussels will go rubbery.

Pork tenderloin with Madeira sauce, salt-baked celeriac & roast shallots

Filet de porc, sauce Madère, céleri-rave au sel et échalotes rôties

Serves six

1–1.2kg pork tenderloin,
   trimmed
1 tbsp vegetable oil
2 garlic cloves,
   finely chopped
2 thyme sprigs
2 shallots, chopped
200ml Madeira
480ml veal stock (see p.245)
2 tbsp butter
Salt and black pepper

Salt-baked celeriac
200g egg whites
   (a carton is fine)
140g table salt
240g coarse salt
1.3kg flour
1 celeriac
Cracked peppercorns
Thyme and rosemary sprigs

Roast shallots
6 whole shallots, unpeeled
1 tbsp vegetable oil
20g butter

Tenderloin is a beautiful cut of pork and this is a special treat, made even more luxurious by the delicious Madeira sauce.

For the celeriac, preheat the oven to 200°C/Fan 180°C/Gas 6. Beat the egg whites, add the salt, flour and 520ml of water, then mix into a dough. Roll the dough out to about 1cm thick. Scrub the celeriac and season it with cracked peppercorns, thyme and rosemary. Place the celeriac on the dough and wrap the dough around it. Make sure it is encased in the dough with no gaps, then bake in oven for 2 hours. Once cooked, remove the crust and cut the celeriac into wedges. Set them aside to finish later.

While the oven is on, prepare the roast shallots. Put the whole shallots in a roasting tin and roast them in their skins in the hot oven (200°C/Fan 180°C/Gas 6) for about 25 minutes, until soft. Leave to cool, then peel off the skins and cut the shallots in half lengthways. Set them aside.

Season the pork tenderloin, add it to a hot pan with the oil and sear it on all sides for about 2 minutes. Put it in a roasting tin with one of the garlic cloves and the thyme and roast it in the oven (200°C/Fan 180°C/Gas 6) for 8 minutes.

Discard the fat from the pan, add the chopped shallots and the remaining garlic, then cook gently until tender. Deglaze the pan with the Madeira, then continue to cook until the liquid is reduced by half. Add the stock and reduce until syrupy, then add the butter, a little at a time, until you have a smooth, slightly thickened sauce.

Heat a tablespoon of oil in a frying pan, add the halved shallots, cut-side down, and the wedges of celeriac and cook until the shallots are caramelised and the celeriac is golden brown. Add the 20g of butter and season with salt and pepper. Carve the pork and serve with the roast shallots, sauce and celeriac.

Caramelised apple pudding, toffee sauce & Chantilly mascarpone

Gâteau de pommes caramélisées, sauce au caramel et Chantilly au mascarpone

Serves six

120g dates, pitted
    and chopped
½ tsp bicarbonate of soda
120g unsalted butter,
    at room temperature
75g caster sugar
2 free-range eggs,
    at room temperature
75g self-raising flour

Apples
150g butter
300g caster sugar
3 large Braeburn apples,
    peeled, halved and cored

Toffee sauce
125g light brown soft sugar
125g dark brown soft sugar
190g unsalted butter
190ml double cream

Chantilly mascarpone
100g whipping cream
100g mascarpone
25g sugar
Seeds from ½ vanilla pod

You will need 6 ramekins
or tin foil moulds, about
5–7cm in diameter

Here's my take on sticky toffee pudding – sheer indulgence!

Place the dates in a pan with 150ml of water and the bicarb. Bring to a simmer and cook until all the liquid has evaporated, then leave to cool. Beat the butter with the sugar in a bowl. Add the eggs and beat until light, then fold in the flour, followed by the date mixture. Spoon into a piping bag and refrigerate.

For the apples, put the butter and sugar in a pan just large enough to contain the apples in one layer. Place over a medium heat and cook to a light caramel, stirring from time to time. Add the apples and a little water and cook, stirring and turning the apples until they are caramelised and soft.

Take the pan off the heat and leave to cool, then remove the apples from the caramel sauce. Continue to cook the sauce to reduce it to a syrupy consistency. Spoon a tablespoon of sauce into each ramekin or mould. Add an apple, rounded side down, and then chill until the apples are cold and the caramel is hard. Pipe the date mix over the apples and set aside.

For the toffee sauce, add both sugars to a pan and caramelise slowly over a high heat. When they have turned to a brown caramel, add the butter, making sure it doesn't burn, then add the cream and cook for a few minutes. Keep the sauce warm.

For the chantilly mascarpone, place the cream and mascarpone in a bowl and add the sugar. Add the seeds from the vanilla pod and whip until stiff.

Preheat the oven to 200°C/Fan 180°C/Gas 6. Bake the puddings for 20 minutes or until the topping feels firm to the touch. Remove them from the oven and leave to cool for 10 minutes. Unmould the puddings into bowls, spoon over some toffee sauce and serve with Chantilly mascarpone.

CHRISTMAS DINNER

Blinis with smoked salmon & créme fraiche (canapé)
Blinis au saumon fumé, crème fraîche

Chicory tarts with Mimolette cheese & chicory salad
Tartes d'endives à la mimolette et salade

Lobster with red wine butter sauce & roast shallots
Homard au beurre rouge et échalotes rôties

Roast duck with Brussels sprouts, Chantenay carrots
& new potatoes
*Canard rôti, choux de Bruxelles, carottes de Chantenay
et pommes de terre nouvelles*

Yule log with Grand Marnier
Buche de Noël, Grand Marnier

Blinis with smoked salmon & crème fraiche (canapé)

Blinis au saumon fumé, crème fraîche

Serves six

200g smoked salmon

Blinis
15g fresh yeast
   or 5g dried yeast
250ml lukewarm milk
150g plain flour
2 eggs, separated
Salt
Vegetable oil

To serve
Crème fraiche
Juice and zest of 1 lemon
1 tbsp chopped dill

Blinis and smoked salmon are a perfect start to our Christmas meal, or any special meal. And if you want to really push the boat out, add a spoonful of caviar as well!

For the blinis, mix the yeast in a bowl with the lukewarm milk and 25g of the flour and leave to prove for 2 hours until frothy. Add the remaining 125g of flour and the 2 egg yolks and whisk to make a batter, then leave to prove again for one hour.

Whisk the egg whites until they form stiff peaks and add them to the batter. Season with salt.

Heat a small (10–15cm) frying pan and add a drizzle of oil. Add a tablespoon of batter and leave until golden brown, then flip it over and brown on the other side. Remove and leave it to cool on a wire rack. You should be able to make about 24 blinis.

Mix the crème fraiche with the lemon juice and zest and the dill. Drape the salmon over the blinis and add a spoonful of the crème fraiche mixture.

Chicory tarts with Mimolette cheese & chicory salad
Tartes d'endives à la Mimolette et salade

Serves six

Chicory tarts
6 heads of yellow chicory
100g unsalted butter
20g caster sugar
375g ready-rolled puff pastry
1 free-range egg, beaten
50g Mimolette cheese or
   mature Red Leicester,
   very finely grated

Salad
2 heads of red chicory
2 heads of yellow chicory

Vinaigrette
5 tbsp olive oil
1 tbsp red wine vinegar
1 shallot, finely chopped
2 tsp Dijon mustard
Salt and black pepper

I really enjoy the combination of the bitter chicory and the sweetness of the Mimolette cheese in these tarts. You can prepare the chicory in advance, then add it to the pastry at the last minute.

Bring a pan of salted water to the boil, add the 6 heads of chicory and cook them until soft. Drain on kitchen paper and squeeze out the excess water, then cut each piece in half.

Melt the butter in a frying pan and add the sugar, then fry the chicory halves until caramelised.

Preheat the oven to 200°C/Fan 180°C/Gas 6. Take the sheet of puff pastry and cut it into 6 rectangles. Carefully score the long sides of each one, about 2cm in from the edge, brush with beaten egg, then fold in the sides. Arrange 2 pieces of chicory on each piece of pastry and brush them with any butter left in the pan. Brush any uncovered pastry with beaten egg and bake in the preheated oven for about 20–25 minutes or until golden and the pastry is fully cooked.

For the salad, mix the vinaigrette ingredients together and set aside. Cut the red and yellow chicory into thin rounds and drizzle with some of the vinaigrette.

Serve the tarts with the salad and the remaining vinaigrette drizzled around them. Garnish with the grated cheese.

Lobster with red wine butter sauce & roast shallots

Homard au beurre rouge et échalotes rôties

Serves six

3 uncooked or
  cooked lobsters
100g butter
Chervil sprigs, to garnish
Salt and black pepper

Lobster is such a luxury and is just the thing for Christmas dinner. If you don't want to cook your own lobsters, you can buy them ready-cooked in some supermarkets now, particularly before the festive season. This dish is made even more of a treat with the rich red wine butter sauce, and the shallots and watercress add the finishing touches.

If you're using fresh lobsters, fill a large pan with about 5 litres of water, bring the water to the boil and add salt. To kill the lobsters, quickly plunge the tip of a sharp knife right below the eyes and cut through to kill it. Place the lobsters into the boiling water, head first.

Cook the lobsters for 9 minutes until the shells are bright red and the meat is cooked but still juicy. Remove the lobsters from the pan, place them into a bowl of iced water and leave to cool for a few minutes.

Crack the lobster bodies and claws and remove all the flesh, making sure you discard any bits of shell. Cut the tail into bite-sized pieces. Heat the butter in a pan, add the lobster meat and toss it through the butter for 3–4 minutes to warm it. Be careful not to overcook the meat, as it will get rubbery.

Serve the lobster with the sauce, a roast shallot and some watercress. Garnish with chervil sprigs

Roast shallots
6 shallots, peeled
50g butter, plus 2 tbsp
500ml vegetable
    or chicken stock
2 fresh thyme sprigs

Red wine butter sauce
600ml full-bodied red wine
1 tbsp red wine vinegar
2 shallots, finely chopped
200ml double cream
250g cold unsalted
    butter, cubed
1 tbsp sugar

Wilted watercress
300g watercress
1 tbsp olive oil

Roast shallots

Put the shallots in a pan with the 50g of butter and the stock, then season with salt, pepper and thyme. Leave them to simmer over a medium heat until the stock is completely evaporated and the shallots are soft and nicely glazed. Cut the shallots in half. Heat the 2 tablespoons of butter in a pan, add the shallots and cook for about 5 minutes until caramelised. Keep them warm until ready to serve.

Red wine butter sauce

Put 100ml of the red wine in a pan with the wine vinegar and shallots and bring to the boil. Continue to cook until the liquid has reduced by half. Add the cream and reduce by a third.

Meanwhile, pour the remaining 500ml of red wine into a separate pan and boil until it has reduced to a syrup. Add this syrup to the pan containing the cream reduction, then lower the heat and gradually whisk in all the diced butter.

You can keep the shallots in the sauce, or if a smoother finish is preferred, pass the sauce through a fine sieve. Season with salt and pepper.

Wilted watercress

Heat a frying pan with the olive oil, then add the watercress and sweat for 30 seconds. Season with salt and pepper and serve immediately.

Roast duck with Brussels sprouts, Chantenay carrots & new potatoes

Canard rôti, choux de Bruxelles, carottes de Chantenay et pommes de terre nouvelles

Serves six

750g new potatoes,
 left whole
1 head of garlic
1 duck, about 1.8kg
Olive oil
100ml white wine
120ml chicken stock
200g Brussels sprouts,
 trimmed
200g Chantenay carrots,
 cleaned
50g unsalted butter
Salt and black pepper

Roast duck is the favourite Christmas bird in our family. It has a celebratory feel and there's all that lovely duck fat for the potatoes! If storing the duck in the fridge, don't cover it, as the skin will then dry out and be nice and crisp when roasted. Remember to remove the duck from the fridge at least half an hour before roasting. Served as part of this Christmas menu, one duck is ample for six, but if you're cooking duck as a Sunday roast, it will serve four.

Place the new potatoes in an ovenproof dish or roasting tin. Crush the head of garlic with your hand to separate the cloves and add them to the potatoes.

Preheat the oven to 220°C/Fan 200°C/Gas 7. Rub the duck with olive oil, season with salt and pepper and place it on top of the potatoes. Pour over the wine and chicken stock and roast for 20 minutes. Reduce the heat to 200°C/Fan 180°C/Gas 6 and continue to cook for another 45 minutes, basting every 10 minutes. If you have a meat thermometer, check that the temperature in the thickest part of the thigh reaches 52°C for perfectly pink meat.

Bring a pan of salted water to the boil, add the sprouts and cook them until tender, then drain and set aside. Cook the carrots until tender and set aside. Heat the butter in a pan, allowing it to brown slightly, then add the carrots and sprouts and season with salt and pepper. Cook until completely soft, adding a little chicken stock if the pan gets too dry.

Remove the duck from the oven, tip out any juices from the cavity and add them to the potatoes.

Cover the duck with foil and leave it to rest for 10–20 minutes. Keep the vegetables warm. Serve the duck with the flavourful potatoes and jus and the carrots and sprouts.

Yule log with Grand Marnier
Buche de Noël, Grand Marnier

Serves six to eight

Ganache
200g dark chocolate
    (70% cocoa solids),
    broken up
200g double cream
Splash of Grand Marnier

Sponge
6 free-range eggs,
    separated
150g caster sugar,
    plus extra for dusting
70g plain flour
30g pure cocoa powder
Pinch of salt
30g butter, melted
2 tbsp icing sugar

Caramelised hazelnuts
About 20 whole
    peeled hazelnuts
250g caster sugar

Wooden toothpicks

The classic yule log is the perfect finale to a Christmas feast.

Start by making the ganache. Put the chocolate in a bowl. Pour the cream into a pan and bring it to the boil, then pour it over the chocolate and mix until smooth. Leave to cool, then add Grand Marnier to taste. Whisk until light and fluffy.

For the sponge, line a baking tray measuring about 30 x 40cm with baking parchment. Preheat the oven to 200°C/Fan 180°C/Gas 6. Beat the egg yolks with 100g of the sugar until pale, then add the flour, cocoa powder and salt, followed by the melted butter. Whisk the whites until frothy, then add the remaining sugar and continue to beat until stiff. Fold the egg whites into the egg yolk mixture, then spread over the baking tray. Bake in the preheated oven for 15 minutes.

Lay a clean tea towel on your work surface and turn the sponge out on to it. Remove the baking parchment. Dust the sponge with a little of the caster sugar, spread some of the ganache over it and roll the sponge up as tightly as possible into a neat log. Leave the sponge to cool, then cover it with the rest of the ganache and leave it to chill in the fridge.

To make the hazelnut decoration, stick a toothpick into each hazelnut and set them aside. Have something ready to stand the toothpicks into while the nuts harden, such as a piece of polystyrene. Heat the sugar in a heavy-based pan until you have a golden-brown caramel. One by one, dip the hazelnuts into the caramel, then stand them in whatever you have prepared and leave them to harden. Drizzle any remaining caramel in a criss-cross pattern over a piece of baking parchment and leave it to harden.

Dust the log with icing sugar and arrange the caramelised nuts on top. Scatter over the pieces of caramel to look like hay.

CHAPTER SEVEN

KITCHEN BASICS

Les basiques

Chicory salad
Salade d'endives

Serves four

3 heads of red chicory
3 heads of yellow chicory
2 oranges
Handful of flatleaf parsley, chopped

Vinaigrette
5 tbsp olive oil
1 tbsp red wine vinegar
1 shallot, finely chopped
2 tsp Dijon mustard
Salt and black pepper

Mix together all the ingredients for the vinaigrette and set aside.

Slice the heads of chicory and add them to the vinaigrette.

Peel and segment the oranges (see page 86), then slice the segments and add them to the salad. Sprinkle with chopped parsley before serving.

Ratatouille

Serves four

1 aubergine
2 courgettes
1 red pepper, peeled and deseeded
1 large onion
2 tomatoes, peeled and deseeded
Olive oil
1 clove of new season's garlic, chopped
1 thyme sprig
2 bay leaves
2 tbsp tomato paste
Salt and black pepper

For this Provençal dish to taste its best, all the vegetables must be cooked separately before being combined for the final stage.

Dice the aubergine, courgettes, pepper, onion and tomatoes – large or small, as you prefer – keeping them in separate piles. Heat about 1cm of olive oil in a pan over a high heat and colour each type of vegetable, except the tomatoes, separately, then drain them in a colander.

Preheat the oven to 200°C/Fan 180°C/Gas 6. Place the aubergine, courgettes, pepper and onion in an ovenproof dish or large pan, then add the diced tomatoes, garlic, thyme, bay leaves and tomato paste. Season and cover with greaseproof paper. Place in the preheated oven for about 20 minutes or until all the vegetables are tender. If you prefer, you can cook this on the hob over a gentle heat. Delicious warm or cold.

Roast carrots
Carottes rôties

Serves four to six

800g carrots, halved or quartered lengthways
4 tbsp olive oil, plus an extra tbsp to drizzle
4 tbsp runny honey
2 tbsp cider vinegar
1 pinch of piment d'espelette or chilli flakes
Leaves from 2 thyme sprigs
2 tbsp finely chopped parsley
Salt and black pepper

Preheat the oven to 200°C/Fan 180°C/ Gas 6. Put the carrots in a large bowl and add the 4 tablespoons of oil, the honey and cider vinegar. Season with the piment d'espelette or chilli flakes, thyme, salt and pepper. Toss to coat the carrots, then transfer them to a baking tray.

Roast for 30–40 minutes until golden. Remove the carrots from the oven, check the seasoning and add the parsley. Drizzle with a little extra olive oil and serve immediately.

Mashed potato with cream
Pommes mousseline

Serves six

1.5kg Maris Piper potatoes
   or other floury potatoes, peeled
200ml semi-skimmed milk
200ml whipping cream
60g unsalted butter, diced
Salt and black pepper

Cut the potatoes into even-sized pieces (not too small). Put them in a large pan, cover them with cold water and add a little salt.

Bring the potatoes to the boil. Skim off any foam that forms on the surface, then reduce the heat to a gentle simmer. Cook until the potatoes are tender, then drain in a colander and leave them to steam dry for a couple of minutes.

Put the milk and cream in a pan with the butter and heat. Put the potatoes through a ricer, then combine them with the liquid, and season. Serve immediately.

Pommes Anna

Serves four

500g King Edward or Rooster potatoes, peeled
5 tbsp duck fat, plus extra if frying
1 garlic clove, finely chopped
1 tsp thyme leaves
Salt and black pepper

Line a baking tin, about 20 x 10cm in size (a small loaf tin is fine), with greaseproof paper. Cut the potatoes into slices, about 2mm thick.

Preheat the oven to 200°C/Fan 180°C/ Gas 6. Melt the fat in a pan with the garlic. Layer the potatoes in the lined dish with a generous amount of fat between each layer. Cover with baking parchment and foil, then bake for one hour until golden and cooked through.

Serve this straight from the oven or leave it to cool, then chill overnight with a couple of weights, such as tins of tomatoes, on top.

If you have chilled the potatoes, remove them from the tin, cut into fingers and fry in a non-stick pan with a little duck fat until golden brown.

Pommes Dauphine

Makes about 20

750g potatoes, peeled
50g butter
Grating of nutmeg
Vegetable oil, for frying
Salt and black pepper

Choux paste
75ml whole milk
50g butter, diced
½ tsp fine salt
75g plain flour, sifted
2 free-range eggs

Cut the potatoes into even-sized pieces and put them in a pan of salted water and cook until tender.

Meanwhile, make the choux paste. Put the milk, diced butter and salt in a pan with 75ml of water and bring to the boil. Take the pan off the heat, quickly add the sifted flour and beat vigorously until the mixture comes together as a smooth paste. Put the pan back over the heat and continue to beat for 2 or 3 minutes. Pour the mixture into a bowl and beat in the eggs one at a time, stirring well until the mixture is smooth.

Drain the cooked potatoes and pass them through a sieve. Add the butter, then the warm choux paste and season with salt, pepper and nutmeg. Shape the mixture into neat quenelles or put the mixture in a piping bag and pipe it into little cylinders about 1.5cm long. You should get about 20.

Half fill a large pan with oil and heat to 180°C. Deep fry the quenelles or cylinders until crisp and golden. Serve at once.

Parisienne potatoes
Pommes de terre parisiennes

Serves two

2 large potatoes, peeled
1 garlic clove, chopped
A few thyme sprigs, chopped
25g clarified butter (see p.234)
Salt and black pepper

Scoop out balls of potato with a Parisienne scoop or a melon baller. Put them in a pan with the garlic, thyme sprigs and 300ml of water. Bring to the boil and cook for about 5 minutes or until the potatoes are semi-soft, then drain.

Add the clarified butter to a frying pan and fry the potatoes until golden, then season to taste. Good with roast meat.

Crushed potatoes
Pommes de terre à l'huile d'olive

Serves four

500g new potatoes
4 tbsp olive oil
3 tbsp chopped chives
Salt and black pepper

Cook the potatoes in a pan of salted water until tender, then drain and peel. Crush the potatoes with a fork, add the oil, chives and seasoning and mix well. Serve at once.

Piccalilli
Condiment
(moutarde et curcuma)

Serves six

100g cauliflower, cut into small florets
100g green beans, cut into 1cm pieces
100g radishes, diced
100g cucumber, cored and cut into 1cm dice
100g red pepper, cut into 1cm dice
25g salt
15g cornflour
1 1/2 tsp turmeric
1 1/2 tsp English mustard powder
1/2 tsp mustard seeds
1/2 tsp cumin seeds
1 tsp coriander seeds
75g caster sugar
250ml white wine vinegar

Place the cauliflower florets, green beans and all the diced vegetables in a large colander over a bowl and sprinkle them with the salt.

Mix well, then cover the bowl with a tea towel and leave in a cool place for 24 hours. Rinse the vegetables in water and drain thoroughly. Set aside.

Blend the cornflour, turmeric, mustard powder, mustard seeds, cumin, coriander and sugar with the vinegar until smooth. Pour the mixture into a pan and bring to the boil and cook until slightly thickened.

Remove the pan from the heat and carefully fold the well-drained vegetables into the hot spicy sauce. Spoon the mixture into warm sterilised jars and then seal immediately. Keep for at least 3 days before using, but this improves with age.

Creamy mushroom sauce
Sauce crémeuse aux champignons

Serves four

2 tbsp olive oil
1 tbsp unsalted butter
400g mixed mushrooms, cleaned
2 garlic cloves, finely chopped
2 shallots, finely chopped
6 tbsp dry white wine
1 thyme sprig
100ml brown chicken stock
400ml whipping cream
2tbsp lemon juice
1 tbsp chopped flatleaf parsley, to serve
Salt and black pepper

Heat the oil and butter in a frying pan and add the mushrooms. Sauté for a few minutes, then add the garlic and shallots and cook until soft. Deglaze with the white wine and leave to reduce until syrupy.

Add the thyme and chicken stock and reduce by half, then add the cream and leave to simmer for another 5 minutes. Season with lemon juice, salt and pepper. Just before serving, add the parsley.

Aioli sauce
Sauce aïoli

Serves six

1 large baked potato
3 tbsp fish stock
Pinch of saffron
6 garlic cloves, finely chopped
2 hard-boiled free-range egg yolks
1 raw free-range egg yolk
200ml olive oil
Salt

Leave the baked potato to cool down to room temperature, then scoop out the flesh and pass it through a sieve. You need 180g of potato for this recipe.

Bring the fish stock to the boil, then take it off the heat, add the pinch of saffron and leave to infuse.

Put the garlic, hard-boiled egg yolks, raw egg and potato in a food processor. Season with salt and process until smooth. Slowly add the oil, a little at a time, adding some of the stock and saffron mixture between each addition. Check the seasoning and transfer to a bowl to serve.

Basic mayonnaise
Mayonnaise de base

Serves four to six

2 free-range egg yolks
1 tbsp Dijon mustard
250ml vegetable oil
250ml olive oil
1 tbsp white wine vinegar
Salt and black pepper

Put the egg yolks and mustard in a bowl and whisk until the mixture is light and creamy. Gradually pour in the oils in a steady stream, whisking continuously and stopping from time to time to make sure the mixture is well emulsified and not splitting or separating.

When all the oil has been incorporated, whisk in the vinegar. This can be kept in the fridge for up to 3 days.

Hollandaise sauce
Sauce hollandaise

Makes about 250ml

250g butter
1 shallot, finely chopped
3 white peppercorns
15ml white wine vinegar
10ml white wine
3 free-range egg yolks
Salt and cayenne pepper
Lemon juice

First clarify the butter. Melt the butter in a pan and bring to the boil. Remove from the heat and set aside to rest, then pass the butter through a sieve, lined with muslin or other fine cloth and placed over a bowl, to remove the white solids. Set aside.

Put the shallot, peppercorns, vinegar and white wine in a pan with 50ml of water, bring to the boil, then reduce by half. Remove from the heat and pass the mixture through a sieve. Discard the shallots and peppercorns.

Mix the egg yolks in a bowl, then add the shallot reduction. Place the bowl over a pan of simmering water and whisk until the mixture has become light and creamy. Take the pan off the heat and add the clarified butter, a little at a time, whisking constantly. Taste the sauce and season with salt, cayenne and a squeeze of lemon juice.

Béarnaise sauce
Sauce béarnaise

Makes about 250ml

1 shallot, very finely chopped
1 pinch of freshly crushed black peppercorns
25ml white wine
25ml tarragon vinegar
250ml hollandaise sauce (see left)
25g fresh tarragon, finely chopped
5g fresh chervil, finely chopped
Salt

Put shallot and crushed peppercorns in a pan, add the white wine and tarragon vinegar, then bring to the boil. Cook until the shallot is soft, then continue to simmer for 4–5 minutes until the pan is almost dry.

Add this reduction and the fresh herbs to the hollandaise sauce and season with salt to taste. Good with steak.

Choron sauce
Sauce choron

Makes about 250ml

10ml white wine
20ml tarragon vinegar
15g tomato paste
20g tomato, diced
250ml hollandaise sauce (see p.234)
Salt and black pepper

Put the white wine and tarragon vinegar
in a pan and add the tomato paste. Bring to
the boil and cook until the liquid is reduced
by half and is the consistency of jam. Add
the diced tomato and simmer for another
couple of minutes. Season with salt and
black pepper.

Mix this through the hollandaise sauce
and season. Good with salmon.

Maltaise sauce
Sauce maltaise

Make about 250ml

Zest and juice of 2 blood oranges
250ml hollandaise sauce (see p.234)
Salt and black pepper

Put the orange zest and juice in a pan
and reduce over a medium heat until
syrupy. Stir this through the hollandaise
and season to taste with salt and pepper.

Good with warm asparagus. You could
add a little more finely grated orange
zest before serving if you like.

White wine butter sauce
Beurre blanc

Serves six

4 tbsp dry white wine
1 tbsp white wine vinegar
2 shallots, finely chopped
250ml double cream
250g cold unsalted butter, diced
½ bunch of chives, finely snipped, to serve
Salt and black pepper

Put the wine, vinegar and shallots in a pan, bring to the boil and continue to cook until reduced by half. Add the cream and boil for one minute.

Lower the heat and gradually whisk in the diced butter, then remove from the heat. You can keep the shallots in the sauce, but if you prefer a smoother finish, pass the sauce through a fine sieve.

Season to taste and mix in the snipped chives at the last moment, or they will lose their colour.

Red wine sauce
Sauce vin rouge

Serves four

1 tbsp olive oil
2 large shallots, finely chopped
1 small bouquet garni
200ml strong red wine
50ml port
500ml brown chicken stock
2 tbsp cold butter, diced
Salt and black pepper

Heat the olive oil in a pan and add the shallots and bouquet garni. Cook for a couple of minutes, then add the wine and port and reduce over a high heat.

When the pan is almost dry, add the chicken stock and continue to reduce until sauce consistency. Remove the bouquet garni, then stir in the cold butter and season with salt and pepper.

Truffle Madeira sauce
Sauce madère à la truffe

Serves four

100ml Madeira
20g truffle, chopped
250ml brown chicken stock (see p.244)
10ml sherry vinegar
1 tbsp cold butter
Salt and black pepper

This sauce goes well with steak or any meat cooked in a frying pan. Once the meat is ready, remove it from the pan and set it aside to rest.

Drain off the fat, put the pan back over the heat and deglaze it with the Madeira. Reduce the liquid until the pan is almost dry, then add the truffle, stock and sherry vinegar. Continue to reduce until the mixture has a nice sauce consistency, then stir in the cold butter and season with salt and pepper.

Pepper sauce
Sauce au poivre

Serves four

½ shallot, finely chopped
½ tsp freshly cracked black or white peppercorns
½ tsp green peppercorns
50ml brandy
100ml brown chicken stock
125ml double cream
Salt

This is a good sauce to serve with steak. Once the steak is cooked, remove it from the pan and set it aside to rest.

Drain off the fat, put the pan back over the heat, then add the shallot and cook for a few seconds. Add the peppercorns, then the brandy. When the pan is almost dry, add the stock and finally the cream, then cook for 2 minutes. Season with a little salt before serving.

Crème pâtissière

Makes about 250ml

4 free-range egg yolks
60g caster sugar
20g plain flour
250ml milk
½ vanilla pod, split

Place the egg yolks and about 20g of the sugar in a bowl and whisk until pale. Sift in the flour and mix well.

Put the milk, the rest of the sugar and the split vanilla pod in a pan and bring to the boil. As soon as the mixture bubbles, pour about one-third of it on to the egg yolks, stirring continuously. Pour the mixture back into the pan and cook over a gentle heat, stirring continuously, for 2 minutes.

Tip the mixture into a bowl and immediately cover with cling film to prevent a skin from forming. Leave to cool.

Classic French dressing
Vinaigrette classique

Serves four to six

1 shallot, finely chopped
1 garlic clove, finely chopped
1 tsp Dijon mustard
1 tbsp white wine vinegar
5 tbsp olive oil
1 chive, chopped
1 chervil sprig, chopped
Salt and black pepper

Put the shallot, garlic and mustard in a mixing bowl and add the vinegar. Slowly drizzle in the olive oil, then whisk until emulsified. Season with the herbs, salt and pepper.

Citrus dressing

Vinaigrette aux agrumes

Serves four

Juice of 1 lemon
2 tsp Dijon mustard
4 tbsp vegetable oil
Zest of ½ orange
Segments from ½ orange
Salt and black pepper

Put the lemon juice and Dijon mustard in a mixing bowl. Slowly drizzle in the vegetable oil, then add the orange zest and segments and season with salt and pepper.

Walnut dressing

Vinaigrette aux noix

Serves two

50g walnut halves
1 tbsp sherry vinegar
4 tbsp walnut oil
Salt and black pepper

Preheat the oven to 200°C/Fan 180°C/ Gas 6. Put the walnut halves on a baking tray and roast them for 5 minutes until lightly toasted. Leave to cool, then chop them roughly.

Put the sherry vinegar in a mixing bowl, then slowly drizzle in the walnut oil. Season with salt and pepper and add the toasted walnuts.

Confit duck leg
Cuisse de canard confite

Makes two

2 large duck legs
600g duck fat
40g Maldon sea salt
1 thyme sprig
1 bay leaf
1 tsp white peppercorns

Trim the duck legs of any excess fat and remove any feathers. Sprinkle the legs on both sides with the sea salt, herbs and peppercorns, then wrap tightly in cling film and leave to marinate overnight.

The next day, preheat the oven to 140°C/Fan 120°C/Gas 1. Brush the excess salt off the duck legs, reserving the herbs and peppercorns. Melt the duck fat in an ovenproof pan, add the duck legs and gently bring the fat to a simmer. Add the herbs and white peppercorns, cover with a piece of baking parchment and cook in the oven for about 2 hours until the meat is tender. The fat must remain at a simmer and not bubble.

To check if the duck is cooked through, try taking the meat off the bone with a knife. If it is done, the meat will come away easily. Leave to cool in the fat and chill or use straight away. If you like, put the duck back in a pan over the heat until the skin is golden and crispy.

Buckwheat pancakes
Galettes de sarrasin

Makes six

100g buckwheat flour
Pinch of salt
1 tbsp butter, melted
1 free-range egg
300ml milk
1 tbsp vegetable oil

Whisk the flour, salt, butter, egg and half the milk in a bowl to make a smooth paste, then mix in the remaining milk.

Heat a pan with a smear of oil. Spoon in just enough batter to cover the base of the pan and cook until the underside is golden. Flip the pancake over to cook the other side, then remove it and keep it warm. Continue until you have used all the batter.

Cornbread
Pain de maïs

Makes one loaf

2 tbsp vegetable oil, for greasing
100g plain flour
100g fine yellow cornmeal
1 tbsp baking powder
1 tsp salt
1 ½ tsp caster sugar
250ml buttermilk
30ml melted butter
2 free-range eggs, lightly beaten
2 red chillies, seeded and finely chopped
100g sweetcorn kernels, tinned or defrosted
1 tbsp sundried tomatoes, chopped
8 basil leaves finely chopped

Preheat the oven to 200°C/Fan 180°C/ Gas 6. Grease a 30cm loaf tin or a traditional clay pot mould with oil.

In a large bowl, mix the plain flour, cornmeal, baking powder, salt and caster sugar, then make a well in the centre.

Mix the buttermilk, melted butter and lightly beaten eggs together, then pour this mixture into the dry ingredients. Stir just enough to combine.

Add the chillies, sweetcorn, sundried tomatoes and basil to the mixture, combine well and pour into the oiled tin or mould.

Bake for 15–17 minutes until the bread is firm to touch. Serve warm.

Langue de chat biscuits
Langue de chat

Makes about 30

125g butter, softened
125g caster sugar
3 free-range egg whites
185g flour
Seeds from a vanilla pod

Put the butter and sugar into a mixing bowl and, using electric beaters, beat until smooth. Add the egg whites one at a time, beating after each addition. Sift in the flour and add the vanilla seeds, then beat until smooth. Cover the bowl and set aside for 20–30 minutes.

Preheat the oven to 190°C/Fan 170°C/ Gas 5 and line a baking tray with baking parchment. Transfer the mixture to a pastry bag with a 1cm plain tip and pipe 5–6cm long 'fingers', on to the tray. Leave at least 2cm between each one.

Bake for about 5–8 minutes or until lightly coloured. Remove from the oven and leave to cool.

Shortcrust pastry
Pâte brisée

Makes enough for 4 small (10–12cm) tartlet shells or 1 x 30cm tart case

200g plain flour, plus extra for dusting
100g unsalted butter, softened,
    plus extra for greasing the tart ring
1 free-range egg
½ tsp salt

Pile the flour on to your work surface and make a well in the middle. Put the softened butter, egg and salt in the well and, using your fingertips, work them together until creamy. Gradually draw in the flour and add a tablespoon of cold water to bring everything together. Do not overwork the pastry. Wrap the pastry in cling film and chill it in the fridge for at least 2 hours before using.

Grease the tin or tins with butter and dust with flour. Roll out the pastry and use it to line the tin or tins, allowing it to overhang the edges. Prick the base with a fork, then line with baking parchment and add baking beans. Leave to rest in the fridge for at least 20 minutes. Preheat the oven to 200°C/Fan 180°C/Gas 6. Bake the pastry for about 20 minutes, then remove the beans and paper and bake for another 10 minutes.

Sweet shortcrust pastry
Pâte sucrée

Makes enough for 1 x 25cm tart case

250g butter
500g flour, plus extra for dusting
Pinch of salt
150g icing sugar, sifted
4 free-range egg yolks

Cut the butter into small pieces and leave it to soften at room temperature.

Sift the flour and salt on to your work surface. Make a well in the centre, add the butter and sugar and gently work them together with your fingertips. Add the yolks and gradually draw in the flour, adding up to 50ml of water as you go.

When the flour has been incorporated, form the dough into a ball, but do not overwork it. Wrap the pastry in cling film and chill it in the fridge for at least 2 hours before using.

Grease the tin with butter and dust with flour. Roll out the pastry and use it to line the tin, allowing it to overhang the edges. Prick the base with a fork, then line with baking parchment and add baking beans. Leave to rest in the fridge for at least 20 minutes. Preheat the oven to 200°C/Fan 180°C/Gas 6. Bake the pastry for about 20 minutes, then remove the beans and paper and bake for another 10 minutes.

Vegetable stock
Bouillon de légumes

Makes about 3 litres

2 large onions, chopped
White part of 1 leek, chopped
½ head of celery, chopped
4 carrots, chopped
2 garlic cloves, chopped
1 tsp black peppercorns
1 bay leaf
A bunch of mixed herb stalks
   (such as thyme and parsley)

Place all the ingredients, except the herbs, into a large pan. Add 3 litres of water and bring to a boil, then cook for 20 minutes.

Add the herbs and simmer for a further 20 minutes. Pass the stock through a fine sieve and use as needed. The stock can be kept in the fridge for up to 5 days or frozen.

Fish stock
Bouillon de poisson

Makes about 2 litres

1kg white fish bones and heads
4 tbsp unsalted butter
1 small onion, roughly chopped
1 celery stick, roughly chopped
60ml dry white wine
6 parsley stalks
1 bay leaf

Remove any gills from the fish heads, then soak the heads and bones in cold water for 3–4 hours. Remove them from the water and chop roughly.

Melt the butter in a deep pan and sweat the onion and celery over a low heat until softened. Add the fish bones and heads and cook for 2–3 minutes, stirring frequently.

Pour in the wine, turn up the heat and reduce by half. Add 2 litres of water and the herbs, then bring to the boil, skimming off any scum frequently.

Strain the mixture through a muslin-lined sieve and leave to cool. The stock can be kept in the fridge for 2 to 3 days or it can be frozen.

White chicken stock
Bouillon de volaille

Makes about 4 litres

2kg chicken bones or wing tips
1 calf's foot, split
1 onion, roughly chopped
1 small leek, roughly chopped
2 celery sticks, roughly chopped
2 thyme sprigs
6 parsley stalks

Place the bones or wing tips and the calf's foot in a large pan, cover with 5 litres of water and bring the water to the boil. Skim off any scum and fat that comes to the surface. Turn the heat down, add the remaining ingredients and simmer for 1½ hours, skimming occasionally.

Pass the stock through a fine sieve and leave it to cool. It can be kept in the fridge for up to 5 days, or you can freeze it.

Brown chicken stock
Bouillon brun de volaille

Makes about 3 litres

2 tbsp vegetable oil
1 large carrot, roughly chopped
1 large onion, roughly chopped
2 celery sticks, roughly chopped
2 garlic cloves, chopped
½ tbsp tomato paste
500g chicken wings, chopped
2 chicken carcasses, cut into small pieces
2 bay leaves
1 thyme sprig

Heat the oil in a large saucepan, add the vegetables and cook until golden. Stir in the tomato paste and cook for a further 5 minutes.

Add 500ml of water, scraping up any caramelised bits sticking to the bottom of the pan. Add the chicken wings and bones and cover with another 4.5 litres of water, then add the herbs.

Bring to a simmer, skim any scum off the surface and leave to simmer for 2½ hours. Pass the stock through a fine sieve and store it in the fridge for up to 5 days or freeze it.

Veal stock
Bouillon de veau

Makes about 3 litres

2kg veal bones, chopped
2kg chicken bones and chicken wings, chopped
1 split calf's foot
½ head of celery, chopped
4 onions, cut into quarters
1kg large carrots, chopped
½ bunch of thyme
½ bunch of rosemary
½ bunch of parsley stalks

Place the veal bones, chicken bones and calf's foot into a large pan. Cover with water and bring to the boil, skimming any scum off the top constantly. Add the vegetables and herbs, then simmer gently for 6–8 hours.

Pass the stock through a sieve lined with muslin, then pour it back into a clean pan. Reduce over a high heat until you have about 3 litres. Pass through a muslin-lined sieve, then store it in the fridge for up to 5 days or freeze it.

Beef stock
Bouillon de boeuf

Makes about 4 litres

2kg beef bones, chopped
2 carrots, roughly chopped
1 onion, roughly chopped
1 leek, roughly chopped
2 celery sticks, roughly chopped
4 garlic cloves, chopped
2 bay leaves
Olive oil
500ml white wine
1 tbsp black peppercorns

Preheat the oven to 220°C/Fan 200°C/Gas 7. Put the bones in a large roasting tin. Add the vegetables and bay leaves and drizzle everything with a little olive oil. Roast for about 30 minutes until the bones and vegetables are brown and caramelised, turning them a couple of times.

Transfer everything to a deep stock pan or a large saucepan, discarding any fat in the roasting tin. Put the tin on the hob and add the wine. Deglaze, scraping up any sticky bits from the bottom of the tin, then add the liquid to the bones in the pan.

Add cold water to cover the bones and vegetables by at least 20cm. Bring to the boil and add the peppercorns, then turn the heat down to a very gentle simmer. Skim well and cook for at least 6 hours. You may need to top up the liquid with a little hot water from time to time to make sure the bones stay covered.

Leave to cool, then skim off any fat and strain the stock through a fine sieve. Keep the stock in the fridge for up to 5 days or freeze it.

RECIPE FINDER

BRUNCH DISHES
Apple turnovers 32
Blue cheese sausage rolls 27
Cheese & ham soufflés 25
Cinnamon rolls 35
Egg, hollandaise & asparagus tartlets 14
Omelette with anchovies 26
Pancakes with honey & fresh berries 31
'Pizza' with figs, goat cheese & ham 22
Potato & sweetcorn waffles with bacon crumb 18
Potato rösti with onion & garlic 21
Prawn French toast with walnut & coriander pesto 17
Venison turnovers 28

SOUPS
Almond gazpacho with pickled peaches 45
Chilled soup with radish tops & nettles 195
Fresh tomato soup 42
Squash soup with roasted seeds 41
Sweetcorn soup 48
Watercress soup with poached egg & black pudding 46

SALADS
Asparagus, tomato & artichoke salad with grilled bread 53
Bitter leaf salad 66
Bulgur salad 196
Chicory salad 228
Courgette salad with olives 50
Dandelion salad with potatoes & bacon
    with quince vinaigrette 49
Heritage tomato salad with anchovies,
    olives & croutons 57
Melon salad with mint & aged balsamic vinegar 54
Quinoa salad with roasted butternut squash,
    pomegranate & citrus vinaigrette 102
Roast cod cheeks with watercress salad 61
Smoked fish salad 58
Summer salad 121

CANAPÉS & STARTERS
Blinis with smoked salmon & crème fraiche 218
Chicory tarts with Mimolette cheese & chicory salad 219
Choux buns filled with pea mousse 186
Creamy mussels flavoured with curry 213
Grilled asparagus with cobnuts 189
Pickled rock oysters 202
Rabbit & pork terrine 203
Smoked eel, beetroot & horseradish cream 210
Smoked trout & salmon mousse tartlets 194

EGG DISHES
Cheese & ham soufflés 25
Egg, hollandaise & asparagus tartlets 14
Omelette with anchovies 26
Omelette with mushrooms, parsley & sheep's cheese 38
'Pizza' with figs, goat cheese & ham 22
Quiche Lorraine 134

PIES & TARTS
Apple turnovers 32
Blue cheese sausage rolls 27
Chicken pithivier with wild mushrooms 125
Chicory tarts with Mimolette cheese & chicory salad 219
Egg, hollandaise & asparagus tartlets 14
Quiche Lorraine 134
Roast vegetable tart tatin 109
Salmon Wellington 114
Smoked trout & salmon mousse tartlets 194
Venison turnovers 28
Venison Wellington with tenderstem broccoli 148

CHEESE DISHES
Blue cheese sausage rolls 27
Braised chicory in ham with béchamel sauce 72
Cauliflower & broccoli gratin with Comté cheese 105
Chicory tarts with Mimolette cheese & chicory salad 219
Truffade 66

PASTA
Creamy onion tagliatelle 68
Linguine with olives, artichokes,
    sundried tomatoes & herbs 71
Tagliatelle with pistou 69
Tagliolini with seafood, pastis & crème fraiche 83

VEGETARIAN (use vegetarian cheese)
Cauliflower & broccoli gratin with Comté cheese 105
Chicory tarts with Mimolette cheese & chicory salad 219
Choux buns filled with pea mousse 186
Courgette gratin 106
Creamy onion tagliatelle 68
Green asparagus with Comté crisps & wild mushrooms 84
Grilled asparagus with cobnuts 189
Linguine with olives, artichokes,
    sundried tomatoes & herbs 71
Quinoa salad with roasted butternut squash,
    pomegranate & citrus vinaigrette 102
Ratatouille 228
Roast vegetable tart tatin 109
Tagliatelle with pistou 69

FISH
Barbecued sea bass with rouille 76
Cod & vegetable parcels 79
Creamy mussels flavoured with curry 213
Gratin with prawns & salmon 113
Grilled marinated mackerel 62
Lobster with red wine butter sauce & roast shallots 220
Mussels Provençal 80
Pickled rock oysters 202
Plaice poached in cider with mussels, scallops & prawns 117
Poached cod with orange & vermouth 75
Provence fish stew with aioli sauce 190
Roast cod cheeks with watercress salad 61
Roasted sea bass 110
Salmon Wellington 114
Sea bream baked in a salt crust 118
Smoked eel, beetroot & horseradish cream 210

INDEX

ACKNOWLEDGEMENTS

This book would not have been possible to make without the wonderful team behind me, always smiling and ready to taste! Many thanks to executive chef Claude Jarczyk for collating the recipes; Nicole Herft and her assistant Simone Shagham for cooking and making the food look beautiful; the ever-professional Cristian Barnett for doing his magic through the lens; Jinny Johnson for her patience and for turning my humble words into food poetry; Smith & Gilmour for the elegant design; Anna Wilkins for sourcing all the dishes and pots; Gaël Combettes for his enthusiasm, inimitable style and panache; and my agent Michael Dean at Andrew Nurnberg Associates.

I'd also like to thank Vicky Eribo and Helen Ewing at Orion for all their support, Hilary Bird for compiling the index and Elise See Tai for proofreading.

And finally the beauty of Saint Rémy and Provence for inspiration.

COOK'S NOTES

All vegetables should be peeled unless otherwise specified.

This is a book about home cooking so there are no complicated cheffy terms, but you might find the following useful.

Blanch: to blanch vegetables, plunge them into a pan of salted, boiling water for a brief period, then drain and transfer them to a bowl of iced water. This stops the cooking process and helps retain the fresh colour of the vegetables.

Bouquet garni: this is a bundle of herbs for adding to soups, casseroles and other dishes. The classic version contains parsley stalks, a bay leaf, thyme, celery and leek, all tied together with string or a piece of leek, to keep them together while cooking.

Confit: the word confit comes from the French confire, which means to preserve. A confit is usually prepared by cooking meat, such as duck, goose or pork, in its own fat and storing it in fat. You can buy confit duck and other preparations or make them yourself. Confit garlic and confit potatoes can be cooked in olive oil.

Deglaze: to deglaze a pan means to add stock, wine or other liquid to a hot frying pan or roasting tin in which food has been cooked. You then stir to loosen any sticky bits from the pan which helps maximise the flavour of the sauce or gravy.

Flambé: this is the process of adding alcohol to a dish and setting it alight to burn off the alcohol content.

Reduce: to reduce liquid, such as stock or sauce, boil or simmer in an open pan so the liquid evaporates by the required amount, intensifying the flavour.

DEDICATION

To all the hungry mouths I have fed and to all those I am yet to feed!

First published in Great Britain in 2023 by Seven Dials
an imprint of The Orion Publishing Group Ltd
Carmelite House, 50 Victoria Embankment
London EC4Y 0DZ

An Hachette UK Company

10 9 8 7 6 5 4 3 2 1
Text copyright © Michel Roux 2023
Design and layout copyright © Seven Dials 2023

A CIP catalogue record for this book is available from the British Library.
ISBN (Hardback) 978 1 3996 1065 0

Publisher: Vicky Eribo
Art director: Helen Ewing
Photography: Cristian Barnett
Design: Smith & Gilmour
Recipe consultant: Claude Jarczyk
Editor: Jinny Johnson
Food stylist: Nicole Herft
Prop stylist: Anna Wilkins
Food stylist's assistant: Simone Shagham
Photographer's assistant: Lisa Paige-Smith
Production manager: Sian Smith

Printed and bound in Italy

www.orionbooks.co.uk